Interior Presentation Sketching for Architects and Designers

MARK ARENDS

Chairman, Industrial Design Program
School of Art and Design
University of Illinois
Champaign, Illinois

VNR VAN NOSTRAND REINHOLD
————————————————————— *New York*

Library of Congress Catalog Card Number 89-5601
ISBN 0-442-20643-7

Printed in the United States of America

Project supervision was done by
The Total Book; Design was
done by Amy E. Becker

Van Nostrand Reinhold
115 Fifth Avenue
New York, New York 10003

Van Nostrand Reinhold International Company Limited
11 New Fetter Lane
London EC4P 4EE, England

Van Nostrand Reinhold
480 La Trobe Street
Melbourne, Victoria 3000, Australia

Nelson Canada
1120 Birchmont Road
Scarborough, Ontario
Canada MlK 5G4

16 15 14 13 12 11 10 9 8 7 6 5 4 3 2 1

Library of Congress Cataloging-in-Publication Data

Arends, Mark W., 1950-
    Interior presentation sketching for architects and designers/
Mark Arends.
        p.   cm.
    Bibliography: p.
    Includes index.
    ISBN 0-442-20643-7
    1. Interior decoration rendering.   I. Title.
NK2113.5.A74 1990
729—dc19

Interior Presentation Sketching
for Architects and Designers

TO MY FAMILY

Contents

Preface

Interior drawing is a specialized form of drawing, just as product rendering, figure drawing, and portraiture are each specialized forms. For one interested in quick and efficient interior sketches either for idea development or for presentations, one needs to understand and control the elements, techniques, and conventions involved in the special case of interior drawing. By considering drawing a design tool rather than an art activity, a designer may lessen the psychological barriers inhibiting his or her drawing development. Also, by focusing only on those aspects of drawing which are useful for interiors, the job of learning drawing or improving drawing skills is made much more consumable, particularly for those with little time to devote to practice.

This text begins at a primer level showing how to use simple drawing skills for idea development and, in a limited way, for presentations. This is to help the reader build confidence and try a number of rendering techniques. The book advances through monochromatic and color interior sketching to full-color interior renderings to set a high mark for those very interested in rendering interiors. By using the text as a program for development from vignette to full renderings, the designer can practice as well as produce useful drawings and can step up to more elaborate levels of drawing as confidence and skills are required. Also in this way, designing and drawing can be seen as parts of the same process which are mutually supportive of each other.

Acknowledgments

The purpose of this text is to present drawing skills and to show how they are used effectively by designers as part of the design process and for the presentation of design concepts. I would like to gratefully acknowledge the following people and design offices for contributing their working drawings for publication in this book:

Chuck Bednar
Jeff Bull
Susan Day
Bob Kloster
Paul Loduha
Jim Prendergast
Jill Roach

Albitz Design Inc., Minneapolis, MN
Armstrong World Industries, Lancaster, PA
Chuck Bednar Design, Oak Park, IL
Earl R. Flansburgh + Associates, Inc., Boston, MA
Eva Maddox Associates, Inc., Chicago, IL
Paul B. Berger and Associates, Chicago, IL
Perkins and Will, Chicago, IL
PHH Avenue, Chicago, IL
Space/Management Programs, Inc., Chicago, IL
Techline, Inc., Champaign, IL
Walter Dorwin Teague and Associates, New York, NY

Drawings reproduced in this text were done by the author unless otherwise noted. In some cases the author's drawing was developed from an underlay by Paul Loduha.

Interior Presentation Sketching
for Architects and Designers

1
Drawing as a Tool for Thinking, Visualizing, and Communicating Ideas

Drawing has always been one of the most versatile and important tools available to designers. In a very broad sense, design drawing is a form of communication with two critical roles: One is to communicate with oneself for the generation and refinement of ideas; the other is to communicate design proposals to other people. As will be discussed later, drawing is well suited to this dual role, and the designer can develop techniques to make drawing a very efficient design tool. Also drawing is a totally visual form of expression and a significant part of an architect's and a designer's work is the creation of visual objects, interiors, and buildings. In fact, the visual quality of their work is the first to be evaluated, long before the performance characteristics of a design project are discussed. This gives drawing a key role in the design process.

Verbal language is very good for making conceptual statements, for pri-

Figure 1–1a
Trompe L'oeil.

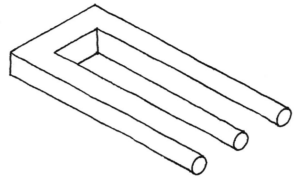

oritizing information, and for communicating this information to others. However, language is awkward and inaccurate when used to describe visual ideas. The three drawings in Figure 1-1 give examples of images which language is powerless to describe. But a designer's work includes both kinds of information, so he or she must develop a visual language to work with and to communicate visual ideas along with verbal skills.

Having both verbal and visual languages to aid in the design process allows the designer to have more creative control of his or her work. A brief look at this design process will help to clarify the roles of these "languages," both verbalization and drawing, for the designer.

Figure 1–1b
Rorschach test.

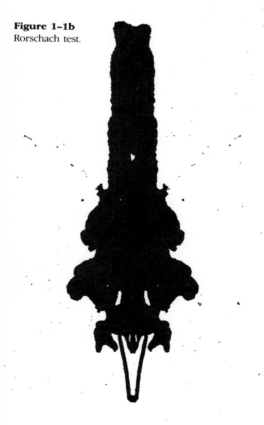

Figure 1-1c
Figure/ground reversal. These drawings (1-1a, 1-1b, 1-1c) are classic examples of visual phenomenon which cannot be adequately described verbally. In a similar way, we can verbally classify interior elements, such as the style of a chair, yet it is impossible to describe the visual impression of such qualities as proportion, shape, and scale.

THE DESIGN PROCESS

The term *design process* is vague and can refer to any and all aspects of creating objects or environments, including client contacts, contract writing, drawing, construction-site visits, and many other activities. This text will deal specifically with drawing which, aside from napkin sketches for clients, is primarily a studio activity. *Design process* as used here refers to primary studio and studio-related activities aimed at generating and refining a concept and preparing a presentation for a client. The initial client contact, contract writing, and preliminary research will be referred to as *predesign activity*. *Postdesign activity* will be used to include the writing of specifications and preparation of detailed plans or transmission drawings for the client or contractor, and any follow-up work done for the design project.

The primary characteristic of any design process is the move from a condition of high ambiguity and low certainty in the beginning, to a condition of low ambiguity and high certainty when the designs are ready to be implemented. For example, in the design of a restaurant there may be some certainty at the outset about the square footage, desired clientele, type of food service, codes, requirements and such; but there is no specific information about the visual design, the floor plan, the atmosphere, and other aspects that the designer is hired to resolve. By the end of the design process, the designer must communicate to the client, as well as to the contractors, suppliers, and inspectors the overall look and design of the restaurant, as well as the exact specifications with which to construct and furnish the facility.

Fortunately both our verbal language and the visual language of drawing allow for ambiguous conceptual descriptions as well as very specific concise specifications (Fig. 1-2). Since they both deal with different kinds of information, they are both useful at different times in the design process, and, at times, they work together as in the common practice of putting notes on drawings or illustrations to be used in a book.

To begin the design process, a strong verbal concept is needed. This is usually referred to as the *problem statement,* and it will be revised many times as ideas are developed. The problem statement is a way of gathering enough intellectual information about the design problem and giving it a focus so the process of visualization can start and will have enough intellectual "fuel" to be resolved in a visual design proposal.

The role of drawing in the design process changes as different types of

Figure 1–2
Room interior. The visual information contained in this drawing would be difficult to describe in a written text. However, some important information which cannot be drawn is included in the form of notes. This visual/verbal language mix is common in the design process. This drawing also shows how loose drawing skills developed in sketching can work in a color presentation sketch. *Louisa Kostich Cowan, Armstrong World Industries, Lancaster, P.A.*

information are needed and as the designer reaches greater levels of resolution of the project. It is important that the designer use different approaches to drawing as well as different types of drawing to foster an appropriate, working visual dialogue both with himself and, when appropriate, with others.

Drawings in the initial, highly ambiguous phase of the design process are characterized by a very loose, sketchy style. These are often called *thumbnail sketches* although they may be large drawings. Typically designers draw freehand, mixing layout or plan drawing with block diagrams, unrelated detail sketches, and lists of ideas or notes. The designer deals with gross issues such as traffic flow and building shape, and mixes these with minor, random thoughts about details for the interior. Figure 1-3 shows an example of this early, divergent phase where the designer tries to generate and explore many different possibilities quickly and, at the same time, clear his or her mind of any preconceived ideas about the project which may inadvertently bias the design work. Both of these tasks are aided when the designer quickly sketches and notes ideas as they come, and then briefly works with the ideas. In addition to helping develop the schematic order of the interior and forming the overall visual design, this phase of loose sketching is also a time when details and bits of information are noted. Some will be discarded, but others will be retained and eventually incorporated in the interior design. This phase may be characterized as dreamlike in that an overall impression of the interior is developed. Some specific details are clear, but if an attempt were made to accurately describe the whole from this impression, it would be disconnected and somewhat nonsensical.

As the designer moves through the design process, he or she performs a number of design methods or skill-based tasks which include sketching, technical drawing, model making, material and structure research, sample selection, and diagraming. These design tasks produce increasingly greater amounts of detail, and the designer becomes more and more specific in identifying elements in the interior. The designer moves from the early, ambiguous phase to the more concise and more specific final phase. The character of the drawings reflect this change, even as they also become more mechanical and clearly-delineated measurements and details for the interior.

The design methods performed by the designer are considered routine tasks because the designer is familiar with them and is very comfortable performing them. The process works something like this: During a moment of decision making, the designer develops a general sense for what design information he is looking and then begins a specific design task, such as drawing. At this point he or she enters a state which can be described as being on automatic pilot, where the brain activity actually lowers. Some psychologists refer to this state as *flow*. As the designer works through a particular task, the information produced from this activity is really a product of the process and the skill level of the designer. These routine activities are part of what is often termed the *visual dialogue* of designers.

Each activity may last for minutes or hours; it goes on until a moment of decision is reached. The work then is evaluated, the information assessed, and that routine activity may be continued or another selected.

This brief look at the design process points out the importance of the designer's ability to utilize a great variety of design methods or tasks. Each method deals with only a limited amount and kind of information which makes variety important. Also, methods only work well when the designer is familiar with them and comfortable performing them, so the designer is recommended to practice. If one has to think through how to perform the methods and how to do the drawing, the chance that a state of flow will be reached is limited and the effectiveness of the visual dialogue between the designer and his or her design activities is compromised.

While acknowledging the importance of drawing as a design tool, an attitude about drawing can be maintained that fosters its use at all levels of design, from the early, ambiguous stages to the final, specific stage. This attitude also helps to develop the skills needed in drawing to make it a comfortable, effective activity in the design process. Some of the skills used in thumbnail sketching can be helpful in developing the skills for making more formal drawings in client presentations.

DRAWING AS A METHOD FOR DESIGNING

Utilizing different forms of drawing will force a designer to consider different aspects of design. Each type of drawing requires the designer to provide certain kinds of information in order to complete the drawing. In a sense the drawing prods and asks questions of the designer, which, in turn, are answered as the drawing is executed. It follows that various completed drawings also communicate different kinds of information. The selection of the form of drawing and the level of ambiguity in the drawing are important

Figure 1–3
Traffic and space plan sketches. These sketches are loose and playful, which is characteristic of the early design phase. *PHH Avenue, Chicago, IL.*

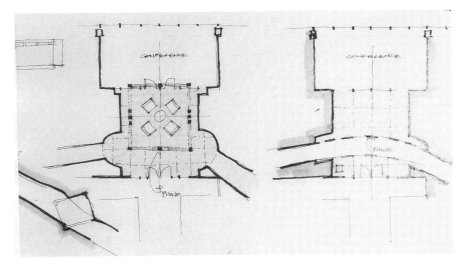

decisions the designer makes, both in working through the design process as well as in making a presentation to the client, or communicating specifications to the contractors. The most common forms of drawing are listed below with a description of their most useful applications.

Thumbnail Sketching

Thumbnail sketching is not really a unique form of drawing but, rather, a drawing activity that has certain characteristics. It is a mistake to underestimate the importance of thumbnail sketching as the drawing styles and techniques used are the foundation for all other types of drawings. Good drawing habits observed in thumbnail sketching will develop later into strong drawing techniques for making presentation drawings.

Many design firms pay particular attention to a young designer's thumbnail sketches when interviewing to fill design positions. Both the quality of the drawings and the range of ideas are deemed important in evaluating a designer's thumbnail sketches. The most notable characteristic of a thumbnail sketch is that it deals with very ambiguous information. As Figure 1-4 shows, it is usually conceptual and can range greatly in subject content. One small sketch may deal with the plan for a mall layout, while another sketch right next to it might be an idea for a planter outside one of the stores. It is useful when doing thumbnails to change drawing forms from orthographic sketching to perspective sketching to diagraming. This encourages different kinds of thinking about the design project. It is also useful to consider the problem at different levels, from the overall plan, perhaps with environmental aspects, to small details such as the style of fixtures to be used. By doing this the designer keeps the whole project in mind and all aspects of the interior will have stronger coordination as the project starts to be resolved and take form. Frequently a detail sketched early in the design process will provide inspiration from the overall style or form of some of the interior elements developed later.

Plan Drawings

A plan drawing is the most common type of design drawing, extremely useful throughout the design process. At the beginning, loose, ambiguous plan sketches can help the designer quickly to consider traffic flow, space

Figure 1-4
Thumbnail sketch. This is a typical thumbnail sketch. It is done quickly and presents ideas ranging from architectural details to space planning. Note the use of line weights even at this early, casual level.
PHH Avenue, Chicago, IL.

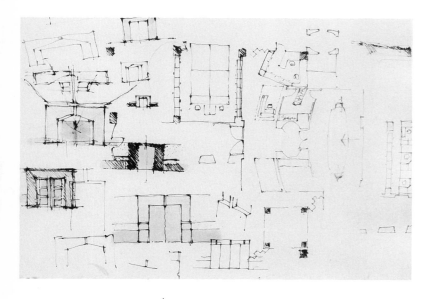

relationships, and interior layouts. Throughout the design process, plan drawings are used to refine design ideas further and to assist in examining layout, proportion, scale, order, position, and measurement (Figs. 1-5a, 1-5b, 1-5c). They also serve as a sort of record-keeping role; as information becomes fixed, it can be drawn accurately into a plan drawing which serves as a summary of the design development of the interior. When a designer wants to see what stage a design project has reached, he or she examines the most recent plan drawing. At the end of the design process, plan drawings form the primary vehicle for transmitting information to the contractors and suppliers. Most other drawing and specifications are keyed to the plan drawings.

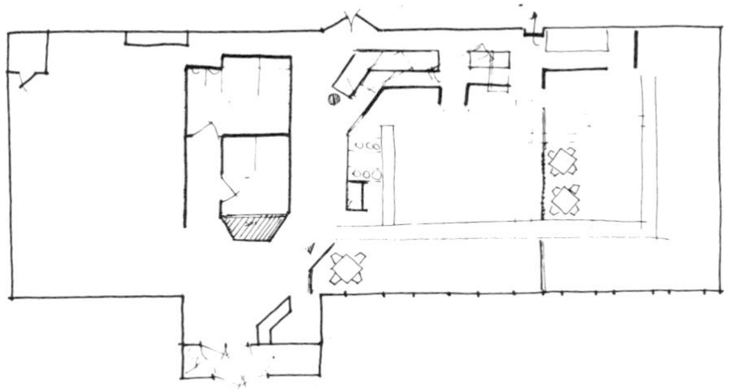

Multiview Orthographics

Commonly referred to as *elevations* and *section views*, multiview orthographics show only the flat layout of an object, interior, or building. Often another view or section drawing is needed to show the depth and three-dimensional quality of the subject. Compared with other types of drawings, orthographics can be done quickly and are excellent for showing the measurements, the scale or relative size of objects in an interior, the layout and

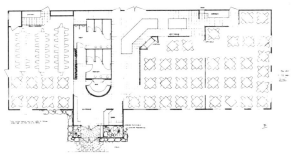

Figure 1–5a
On this early, loose floor plan, only the exterior walls and door locations are fixed

Figure 1–5b
This mid-project floor plan has fixed the windows, seating areas, and traffic flow.

Figure 1–5c
On the final floor plan, only the colors, materials, and furnishings are sill in flux. Each of these plan drawings (Figures 1-5a, 1-5b, 1-5c) represent both an exploration of the design problem and a summary of fixed design ideas. As elements become fixed, they are added permanently to the plan drawing. Ideas which still are being explored are sketched loosely and will change from one plan to the next.

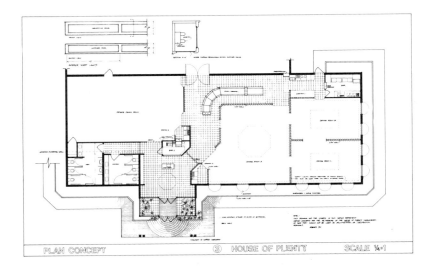

PLAN CONCEPT   ③ HOUSE OF PLENTY   SCALE ¼=1

arrangement of a wall surface, as in Figure 1-6, and the proportion, and the graphic qualities of a surface or entrance way. It is very common to draw façades of buildings, interior walls, and entrance ways with orthographic elevations. These elements are usually in low relief as the dimensional volume of an interior is primarily space, and many of the architectural elements are essentially flat. This makes the design of these elements very much of a graphic-design problem involving the arrangement and use of material, color, texture, and such. Because orthographics can be dimensioned, they make excellent transmission drawings to instruct the contractors and to key to the plan drawings.

Figure 1-6
Elevation drawings of interior walls, like this one, show the layout and measurement of a surface. In that way they are excellent drawings for solving graphic organization problems.

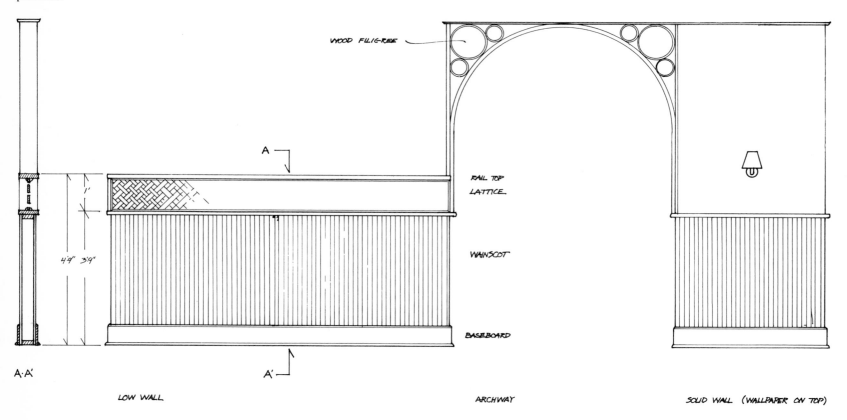

WOOD FILIGREE

A

RAIL TOP
LATTICE.

WAINSCOT

BASEBOARD

4'9" 3'9"

A·A'

A'

LOW WALL

ARCHWAY

SOLID WALL (WALLPAPER ON TOP)

Parallel-Line Drawing

Parallel-line drawings are used to show three-dimensional volumes and are easily constructed with parallel lines. They include isometric, diametric, trimetric, axonometric, and oblique drawings and have the common characteristic of showing the adjacent sides of an object, usually the top, front, and one side. Because all parallel lines of an object are drawn parallel on the paper, there is no perspective illusion. Parts of the object appear out of scale: the back of the object appears too large while the front appears too small. These drawings show a sense of the true three-dimensional volume of an object or space as well as the relative position of each element to each other in the space.

Parallel drawings give the impression of a three-dimensional block diagram and clearly show the object in a space, as well as show a plan view of that space. They are not very effective, however, at showing a realistic view of an interior; perspective is much better for that as can be seen in the office plan in Figure 1-7. Parallel-line drawings are difficult and seem to be unnatural to sketch, but they are very easy to construct mechanically and therefore are commonly used as part of a formal presentation.

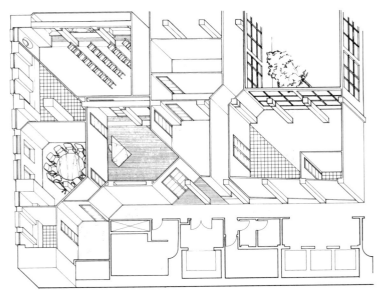

Figure 1-7
Axonometric plan for an office space. This drawing shows the relative volume and position of elements in the interior. It also shows the floor plan well. However, an axonometric drawing does not convey the same feeling for space that a perspective will. *PHH Avenue, Chicago, IL.*

Perspective Drawings

As with orthographic and plan-drawing perspective, drawings can be quick, freehand sketches or elaborate, accurate-presentation drawings. Accurate-perspective drawing is the most difficult and time consuming type of drawing to execute. It offers the most convincing or realistic view of an interior (Fig. 1-8). Fortunately, once a designer understands the formal rules of perspective drawing and is familiar with some of the perspective "tricks" presented in Chapter 4, to execute convincing perspective sketches, to use either for working drawings or for presentation, is not difficult. The best use of perspective is to present a realistic view of an interior. Perspectives are very good for showing volume and the spatial relationship of objects to each other, for conveying the visual and psychological impression of a space, and for working out the details of form and the relationship of the parts to each other.

Being aware of the dynamics of drawing both as a design tool for developing ideas and as an indispensable aid for communicating design concepts will help to make the selection of the type of drawing most appropriate to the situation easier. It will also assist the designer to master effective drawing skills. The designer should plan the design process to allow time for exploring drawing, for trying unfamiliar techniques; not only will drawing skills improve but confidence will be gained in the design work.

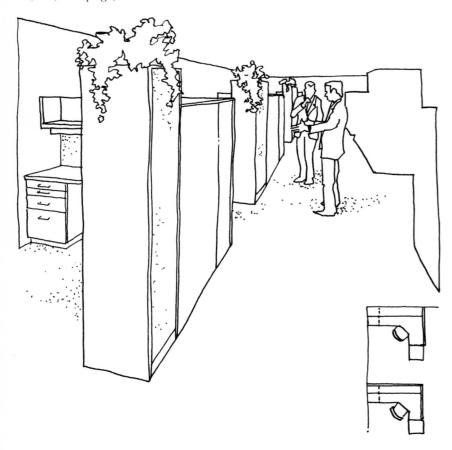

Figure 1–8
Perspective view of a proposed office space. Even this simple perspective line drawing can be effective in putting the viewer into the space. *Paul Loduha, Techline, Inc., Champaign, IL.*

2
Elements of Drawing

Each of the various types of drawing discussed in Chapter 1 (orthographic, perspective, plan and parallel-line drawing) can be executed at a simple level, requiring little time or preparation or at a complex, highly-detailed level where a considerable amount of preparation and time is required. At any level these types of drawings are useful both in the development of design ideas and in the presentation of design concepts to a client.

Regardless of the type of drawing, there are certain elements in a drawing which contribute to its success and usefulness in a presentation. When handled properly these elements give a drawing a good surface quality or visual appeal. Many designers refer to a highly controlled design drawing or rendering as being "slick." This chapter discusses the basic elements of design drawing that contribute to the drawing's visual appeal and presents some techniques which help develop a good surface quality.

LINE QUALITY

Perhaps the most important element of a drawing is line quality. While there are many ways to make lines on paper, it is important that whatever drawing technique is used be used consistently.

Generally line drawings can be categorized into one of two groups: gestured lines and drawn lines. Gestured lines are most common in loose sketches and thumbnail drawings. Traced or carefully drawn lines are used to produce more tightly controlled formal drawings.

Gestured Lines

To make an effective gestured line, the designer should consider the line to be one stroke made with the hand and the arm. The wrist should be almost locked. Visualize where the line should go, where it starts and where it ends, and then, with one quick stroke, the line is put down. It may help to gesture the line in the air just above the paper a few times to get the feel of the gesture; then draw the line. For example, to make an ellipse, the designer first visualizes it, circles it in the air, then with one quick stroke puts it on the paper. If he or she "stutters" the line by drawing it a few times directly on the paper rather than in the air, the resultant collection of lines gives a rather fuzzy, shabby look to the drawing. Stuttered lines, as shown in Figure 2-1, also give the appearance of being inaccurate and do not convey the sense of confidence and crispness that is desired in a design drawing. The following points may help a beginner to develop effective gestured lines.

A gestured stroke should feel the same for all lines regardless of the direction of the stroke. It may help to have one finger lightly touch the paper as the lines are drawn. This helps to control the weight of the line, giving better control over the amount of pressure being used in putting the pen to the paper. Generally a light stroke is desired. Also by locking the wrist and moving the hand and arm together, the stroke and, subsequently, the lines are straighter and do not arc or curve because of the hand pivoting at the wrist or elbow.

▶ When drawing a series of parallel lines, draw in one direction only rather than in a back-and-forth motion. This will produce a more consistent and more accurate line. It will also reduce the tendency to be lazy and scribble lines on the paper.

▶ A line should have a visible beginning and end. Press, or pause if using a felt-tip pen, a little harder at the beginning and the end of each stroke. One may even make a definite dot at the end of a stroke. When someone views a drawing, the viewer's eye runs along the lines very quickly; upon reaching the end of a line, however, the direction of

Figure 2-1
Stuttered lines, like the ones used in this drawing, do not convey a sense of confidence or the crispness desired in a quick sketch.

travel changes, and these heavier points define those stopping points and the change in direction, or, in terms of the drawing, the corners of the objects (Fig. 2-2).

▶ Along with having a stronger beginning and end to a line, the weight of a line should vary. It should be heavier at the ends and thin or light along its length. This will occur naturally if the ends are emphasized and the line is gestured quickly. Also, throughout the drawing the line weight should vary. This helps the viewer read the drawing as volumetric objects in three-dimensional spaces. Typically objects closest to the viewer are drawn with bolder, heavier lines, and those farther away are drawn with lighter lines and less detail. Also, the lines used to draw an individual object should vary; edges which overlap other objects or spaces should be heavier, and those in which both surfaces creating the edge can be seen should be lighter.

▶ Trying to gesture a complex curve in one stroke can be very difficult. Usually it is easier and more accurate to break the complex curve into a series of simple curves, each of which can be gestured quickly with a single, consistent stroke which does not require changing direction in the middle of the stroke. Figure 2-3 gives an example of the way in which curves can be shown with a series of quick-gesture strokes.

▶ To emphasize the termination of a stroke, many designers "punctuate" a gestured line by pausing at the end of the stroke to leave a dark dot. Some even put a period at the end of a stroke by picking up the pen and, with a quick motion, dotting the paper.

Drawn Lines

A drawing line is made more slowly than a gestured line. It is the line used when tracing or darkening faint lines on a paper. This kind of line usually has a uniform line weight, value, and texture. By controlling these elements of a drawn line the designer can produce line drawings which are effective for use in presentations.

Line weight or thickness helps the viewer to clearly distinguish among various objects in a drawing, and it enhances the illusion of three-dimensional space. Figure 2-4 demonstrates a very simple rule about line weights that serves as a good foundation for manipulating line weights: When the

Figure 2–2
This sketch was done in a quick, gestured style. The end points of each line are strong which emphasize the corners.

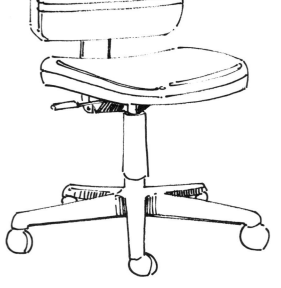

Figure 2-3
The lines used to draw this chair consist of a series of quick-gesture strokes put together to make complex curves.

drawing shows the two surfaces of an object that create an edge, the line used to show that edge is light. Where only one surface adjacent to the edge is visible, the line used to show that edge is heavy. If the surfaces of two objects are in contact, the line separating them is of medium weight.

Chapter 5 will show how line weight can be manipulated for subtle effects or for dramatic, pictorial composition.

To produce the different line weight, it is convenient to use different size felt-tip pens or markers. Two line weights can be made with each pen by using a light or a heavy touch, but to really control the line weight, it is best to a use a fine-, medium-, and bold-tip pen.

A bold art marker can produce a number of heavy strokes, depending upon which edge of the felt tip is used. For a very crisp, heavy line a calligraphy pen is excellent; it makes a uniform line with a squared-off end rather than the rounded, blunt end left by most felt tips. Figure 2-5 shows the crisp edges that can be achieved with the designer's use of a calligraphy pen.

Figure 2-4
A variety of line weights are used in this drawing to enhance the perception of depth and volume in the drawings. *Paul Loduha, Techline, Inc., Champaign, IL.*

Figure 2-5
Calligraphy pens were used in these drawings to enhance the line weights and add a crisp edge to the objects being drawn.

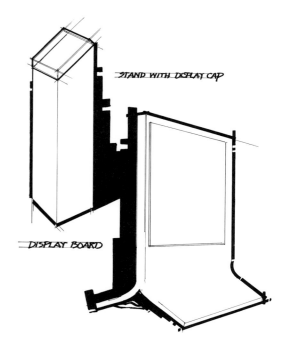

STAND WITH DISPLAY CAP

DISPLAY BOARD

Line value refers to the darkness of a line, ranging from a faint gray to a deep black. For the purposes of design drawing line value also may refer to the color of a line, since most lines are within the color range of a very warm gray, almost a brown, to a cool, bluish gray. Perhaps the most common use of line value is in setting up a drawing. By using a light gray, fine-point marker when sketching an interior, and then, once the composition is complete, going over the sketch with a darker marker, the light construction lines nearly seem to disappear and add a light tonal value to the drawing. With this technique designers can visualize the finished drawing before any dark lines have been used and reposition or correct perspective errors (Fig. 2-6). Once the final dark lines are put down, the light-value pen can be used to plan the addition of detail element to a drawing.

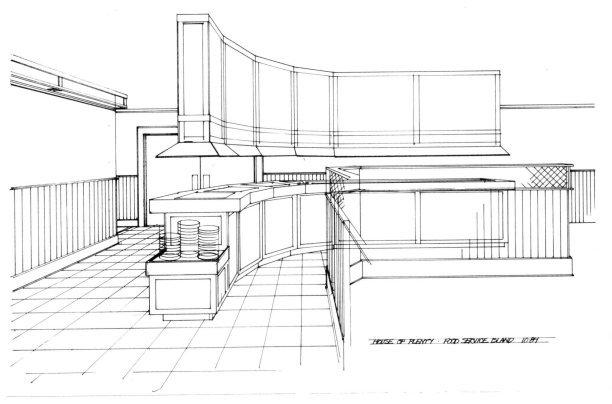

HOUSE OF PLENTY · FOOD SERVICE ISLAND 10·84

Figure 2-6
The bold-line work in this drawing overpowers the light construction lines, allowing them to virtually disappear.

Line value and color also can enhance the illusion of perspective space. Generally light and middle gray tones are used at the deepest part of the perspective space and at the outside edges of the drawing. Strong contrasts of dark and light gray shades are used in the foreground and at the focal point or point of interest in the drawing. Likewise cool gray colors are used at the back and sides of the drawing while warm gray colors pull the viewer's attention to the focal point and foreground.

Line texture or the character of a line is determined by how the line is made. There are two basic types of textured lines. One is a crisp, hard-edge line made by drawing along the edge of a drawing guide, often called a straight-edge drawing. The other is a freehand line, often drawn or traced, but sometimes gestured. The specific texture of a line can be the natural texture of the lines produced by the designer's unself-conscious drawing, or the texture may be made very deliberately with the designer consciously employing a technique to produce it as the carpet shown in the illustration in Figure 2-7. The texture of the lines used in a drawing should be consistent throughout the drawing regardless of the line weight or the size of the objects drawn in the interior, or if the lines are straight or curved. This suggests that there are advantages and drawbacks to both straight-edge drawing and freehand drawing.

Figure 2–7
A textured line may be used to indicate carpet and other interior surfaces.

Straight-edge drawing employs the use of a variety of guides, T squares, triangles, circle and ellipse guides, French curves, ships and flexible curves, and a variety of templates. This technique is almost always used for floor plans, elevations, and other parallel-line drawings. The primary advantages of straight-edge drawings are in accuracy and speed. The edge of the drawing guide acts as a line itself to allow the designer to position the line on the paper before ink is put down by running the pen along the edge of the guide. The line also can be made very quickly and accurately as the guide keeps it from going astray. By using different pens and controlling the pressure used on the pens, a variety of line weights and values can be achieved. Various textures can also be introduced to straight-edge drawing by the following methods: using a textured paper, putting a textured sheet under the thin layout paper the drawing is on, using guides with a rough edge such as a torn card stock, or deliberately jiggling the pen in some manner. To draw the basic layout and construction of an interior perspective, straight-edge drawing is fast and accurate; however, to repeat lines, to draw details, small objects, or soft or irregularly-shaped objects in the interior, straight-edge drawing can be very slow and tedious. For this reason straight-edge drawing often is used to set up a perspective, by drawing in the basic interior architecture and locating the major elements in the interior. That drawing then is used as an underlay and traced freehand. The smaller elements are added later. Once the interior composition is complete, a final overlay can be made and a careful freehand tracing done with the desired texture, values, line weights, and added color. For some interiors in which most of the elements are rectilinear, and there is no need to draw small objects, a straight-edge drawing can be done easily for the presentation.

As mentioned previously, the most common use of freehand-line work in a presentation drawing is to trace over other lines, either on a separate sheet on an overlay or directly over the lines of a lighter value. Two advantages for using a freehand line are to easily control a variety of textures and to add details without tedious perspective construction. Because the drawing has a freehand look to it, minor errors in perspective are overlooked by the viewer. The drawing is not expected to be as accurate as a straight-edge drawing which looks to be very precisely drawn. Because a uniform-surface quality is desired in a drawing, the technique used to make freehand lines must be consistent throughout the drawing, regardless of the pen used. A rough, uneven texture in one area of the drawing will not be compatible with a smooth, hand-edge line in another part of the same drawing.

Figure 2–8
Boat interior. The focal point in this drawing is rendered carefully while other elements are left as line drawings which fade to the edges of the paper. *Chuck Bednar, Chuck Bednar Design, Oak Park, IL.*

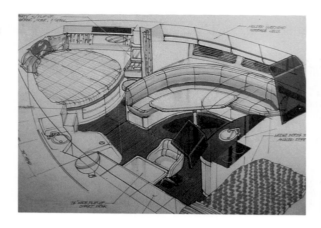

FIGURE-GROUND

Figure ground refers to the relationship between object and surfaces; that is, when something appears to be the object or subject of the drawing and commands the most visual attention, it is the *figure*, and other elements will appear to be the *background* for the subject in a particular drawing. In the design of an interior some elements in a drawing are dominant and others are supportive or neutral as is demonstrated in the rendering of the boat interior in Figure 2-8. Likewise a perspective drawing of an interior should emphasize the dominant elements and de-emphasize the neutral elements. A drawing in which all aspects of an interior are shown to be the same tends to be lifeless and does not present the design ideas well. Emphasize the dominant design elements of a drawing by use of high contrasts in line and value; by use of strong colors; and by overlapping the less important elements, positioning them to the center of the drawing, and drawing in more detail on these elements. It also helps to focus attention on a particular part of a drawing by adding the figure of a person who is interacting with, or looking toward, the important elements of the interior drawing. De-emphasize elements in a drawing with neutral color and more values, light lines and less contrast, and by fading the drawing out at the edges of the page.

Figure 2–9
High contrasts can be used to compose boldly on interior.

CONTRAST

Contrast, an often overlooked element in a drawing, is one that when used properly can make for a very dramatic, powerful composition. Strong contrasts can be used to attract the viewer's attention to important areas of the drawing. As can be seen from the high contrasts in Figure 2-9, contrasts also help to enhance the perception of three-dimensional space in a drawing. Effective contrasts can be created in a composition by alternating light with dark on a surface; a light surface will contrast with a dark surface and vice versa. For example, in drawing a chair against a wall, the wall may be fairly dark, or if not the whole wall, just the shadow area of the chair may be dark, and the chair drawn in outline or with a very light value.

Another good rule of thumb for creating and controlling contrast is to assign a common relative value to the surfaces in the interior that face the same direction. For instance, the surfaces that face up where the strongest light source usually comes from, should be light. Surfaces that face the left are a medium value, and surfaces that face right are the darkest value. A very simple yet effective use of contrast is to render the surfaces in a line drawing that face away from the light source, as to the right-vanishing point in two-point perspective, a light gray. Even this minimal, low contrast will push the light surfaces forward visually and give the drawing a greater sense of space as well as a more dramatic visual presence. Figure 2-10 demonstrates how the appearance of greater volume is achieved with this light contrast technique.

Figure 2–10
By putting a light value on all surfaces facing the same direction in a line drawing, a greater sense of volume is achieved in the drawing.

Figure 2-11
Eye-level view of an exhibit
set in an interior space.

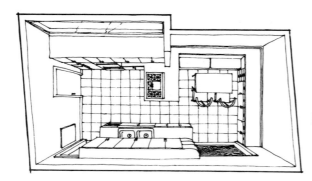

Figure 2-12
Bird's-eye view of a kitchen.

COMPOSITION

The final significant element in a design drawing is composition. This is the choice of view, the positioning on the page, and the use of auxiliary drawing and information to effectively present a design concept. The choice of composition and the layout of the drawing should reflect the purpose the drawing will serve. The most common choice of view in a perspective composition is to look directly into a room, at eye level, with the focal point of the interior in the center of the page. This is a very serviceable and convenient choice for most interior drawings. However, since one drawing cannot convey all of the different kinds of information important to the design of an interior, other compositions and points of view allow the designer to show specific design information efficiently or to highlight design elements in an interior. The following list presents a few of the most common compositional alternatives available to a designer by using perspective and the kind of information the compositions are most effective in describing.

▶ Eye-level view of an interior. This view, from which Figure 2-11 is rendered, is intended to give the viewer a sense of being in the interior, to see what it will look like when the room is constructed. Because this view can show only a small portion of the interior effectively, usually less than half, it often is used to focus on the most important design elements in the interior. This may be the architectural treatment, a furniture grouping, or the play of textures, colors, and furniture styles in the interior.

▶ A bird's-eye view of an interior. This is often fairly easy to construct once the floor plan is drawn, and shows the interior in a novel way (Fig. 2-12). This view can be thought of as an enhanced floor plan where traffic flow, space plan, and location of interior elements becomes very clear. While this view does not put the viewer into the interior, it does a good job of showing the working plan of the interior as well as the character of the furnishings. See Figure 2-13 for a worm's eye view of a bank lobby.

▶ Collage, a composition technique, allows the designer to present detailed information about an interior. Normally there is a major drawing, either a floor plan, an elevation, or a perspective, and a series of detail drawings that show specific parts of the interior. These detail drawings are keyed to the major drawing and may show a construction detail, a material or furniture choice, an alternative design, or any of a number of design specifics. In Figure 2-14, the designer has shown two views and color variations of masking units for a bowling center.

LETTERING

An often overlooked and underestimated part of a drawing is its lettering. While lettering is usually the last consideration when sketching or making a presentation drawing, it does identify the subject of the drawing, the job, and the design office. Lettering also can be used to call out such specifics in the drawing as materials, the way in which something works, and other notes on the performance of an element in the interior. The first consideration when adding lettering to a drawing is that the lettering be consistent and look confident. Most designers will develop their own style of lettering, but whatever their style, six characteristics of lettering should be common

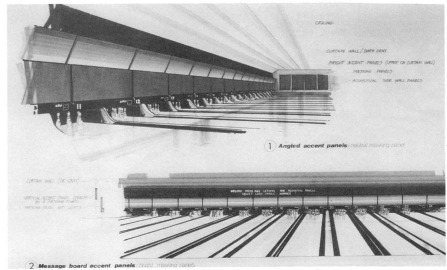

Figure 2–14
Collage showing two views and color variations of masking units for a bowling center.

Figure 2–13
Worm's-eye view of a bank lobby.

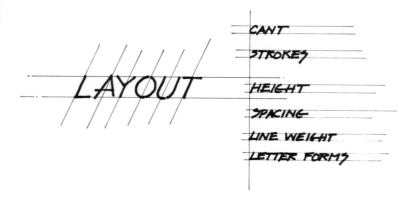

Figure 2-15
Consistent lettering is important if it is to be used on drawings. This diagram shows the six basic components of lettering.

Figure 2-16
Transfer lettering can be traced to produce outline lettering for title blocks.

to all lettering. These include controlled and consistent letter height, cant, stroke or gesture, letter spacing, line weight, and letter form and are demonstrated in Figure 2-15.

▶ Letter height should be consistent and even. It is common to draw two light, parallel guidelines and do the lettering between them. With practice, both uppercase and lowercase lettering can be used with this technique.

▶ The cant or slant of each letter should be the same. This can be seen by drawing a light line through the height of the letter along the vertical axis or stroke.

▶ Each letter can be seen as a combination of a series of strokes, made with the same gesture each time. These gestures are a vertical, horizontal, right and left diagonal, and right and left curve.

▶ Letter spacing is a more difficult element to gain control over; it is, however, easily noticed when wrong. Most people generally will use too wide of a letter spacing. Compare the letter spacing of a typewriter with that of a printed page. The typewriter spacing is too wide and mechanical looking where the typeset-page spacing is usually much closer, and the word patterns are easier to read.

▶ Line weight depends upon the size of a letter. In general, the larger the lettering, the heavier the line weight needed. Lettering line weights also should be compatible with the line weights used in the drawing; usually lettering used within the picture plan is lighter, and lettering used in the title block is heavier.

▶ The form of an individual letter should be consistent throughout. For example, no matter how one chooses to make the letter *A*, all letter *As* should have the same form. Also, the form of a letter should be compatible with the form of the other letters, not usually a problem if the gesture used to stroke the letter parts is consistent.

Another technique to use for lettering titles on drawings is to trace presstype and create a freehand-outline drawing of the letter forms (Fig. 2-16). Since these letters are drawn, they relate to the character of the sketch better than will the transfer lettering, which looks too mechanical and self-conscious for casual sketches.

SOURCES FOR QUICK PERSPECTIVE DRAWINGS

There are a number of aids to drawing in perspective to make the process go faster. They also can add details that would otherwise be left out by the designer for the lack of time to draw them. All of the following are really forms of tracing and modifying conventional elements common to most interiors.

▶ Morgue file. This is a collection of photographs and drawings from magazines and other sources which may be useful for an interior project. The morgue file can be divided into two sections: one contains images that suggest design ideas for interiors to be used as visual reference material; the other section contains interior elements that may be traced into a drawing. Probably the most useful file is one that contains people in various poses and sizes. These figures can be placed under the drawing paper and stylistically traced into the drawing. It is helpful when adding to this file to measure the figure in the photograph or drawing and indicate the size and scale. In a perspective sketch the designer may be looking for a 4-inch figure or, for an elevation, a twelfth-scale figure, and if the file figures are marked, locating the appropriate one is quick and simple. Other morgue files could be established for cars, furniture, light fixtures, and drapery to serve as tracing material or to show the visual character, making it easier to draw or suggest the items in the interior drawing.

▶ Clip art. A morgue file is really a collection of homemade clip art because both are used in a similar way. The most useful clip-art books are those containing drawings of furniture groupings as, for example, the illustrations in Figure 2-17, used primarily in newspaper advertising. These underestimated drawings show a simple, effective style of drawing which can be imitated or referred to by the designer to learn how to draw material, texture, and patterns common to interior furnishings. Clip art is also useful in constructing an interior; for example, a room setting of furniture depicted in clip art can be enlarged on a photocopy machine. The vanishing points are located by extending the perspective lines and a room is built around the furniture. Then, with an overlay or a series of overlays, the interior can be modified and detailed as desired.

Figure 2-17
Clip art from newspaper advertising can be expanded into a perspective drawing. The furniture can be modified to match the desired style.

► Photographs. Polaroids, slides, and photographic prints of an interior make ready perspective layouts for sketching. A photograph of the interior space to be worked on, or a space similar can be enlarged and converted into a line drawing by using a lucigraph or any number of photo mechanical processes, or by tracing. It is helpful to put a scale into the interior before photographing such as tape lines on the wall and floor at one foot intervals. These markings then can be projected and made into a grid in the line drawing to provide perspective references for changing the interior. If there is a very large interior or an expanse of space to be dealt with, a plan view of the space can be photographed with a vertical scale for height references. First photograph the plan drawing and reference scale at a low angle, enlarge the photograph to a comfortable working size, and then make the line drawing. Such vertical lines for the interior as corners and columns can be projected up vertically from the floor plan, and the horizontal measurements will be determined by the vertical reference scale traced from the photograph.

► Commercial grids. Perhaps the most common type of perspective aid is a prepared grid available from art stores in a variety of perspective formats suitable for drawing buildings, interiors, and products. While the perspective grid limits the designer's choice of view and composition of the drawing, it does allow for a very fast positioning of elements in the interior, and the vanishing points used to make the grids are far enough apart to give a convincing interior view. The positioning of vanishing points will be discussed further in Chapter 4.

3
Nonperspective Presentation Sketches

As mentioned in Chapter 1, there are a number of nonperspective- or parallel-line-drawing systems that are very useful to the designer. These systems do not represent buildings, interiors, or objects with the same illusion of real space that perspective drawing does; rather they present a more abstract view of the subject as does a plan or a diagram. Because parallel-line drawings, compared to perspective drawings, are relatively quick to produce, it makes sense to utilize them in a presentation whenever possible. To that end there are some techniques that can be used to enhance parallel-line drawings so they are more easily identified as depicting three-dimensional space.

Floor plans and elevations are the two types of parallel-line drawing most commonly used by designers as they readily lend themselves to modification to suggest perspective space.

Using a reproduction machine, a floor plan or an elevation easily can be copied and the copies modified for presentation. It is important always to think of floor plans and elevations in terms of the three-dimensional space they represent so that it is easier and less confusing to manipulate the drawings to suggest depth.

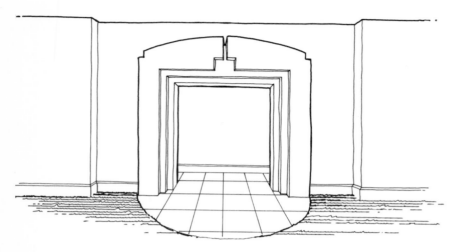

Figure 3–1
An elevation can be adjusted
with the addition of a vanishing point to make a shallow,
stagelike perspective. In this
drawing the walls have been
moved slightly to form the
shallow perspective and the
floor has been exaggerated
to suggest more space.

LIMITED-PERSPECTIVE PROJECTION

Floor plans and elevations are used in a number of perspective-construction systems for full perspective drawings. This is usually a complex, time-consuming drawing process. For major drawings in a presentation, this process is justified; however for support drawings it is too costly a process. Floor plans and elevations also can be used to produce shallow-type drawings with very little effort on the part of the designer. The resultant drawings are stagelike because of foreshortening of perspective space, but even with that limitation there is enough depth suggested in the drawing to help the viewer understand the plan or elevation in three dimensions. One might compare the spacial quality of these drawings to that of a pop-up book; indeed, the technique is similar. Essentially, surfaces on different planes are moved slightly forward in one-point perspective. Because the movement is slight, the perspective lines can be estimated and drawn in without using an elaborate measuring or construction system. Figure 3-1 is an example of the way an elevation can be adjusted for this shallow perspective.

The following steps are typical of this process:

1. Make several copies of the original elevation or floor plan to work from.

2. Above the elevation on one of the copies, draw the plan view of that elevation to serve as a guide for moving forwards or backwards in the pictorial space.

3. Select a vanishing point and mark it as the drawing. This may be in scale at eye level on the elevation. Then draw perspective lines through the corners of the plans to be moved forward or backward.

4. Position a sheet of tracing paper over the elevation and trace the main section of wall. Then shift the tracing paper slightly to allow for the foreshortened surface or space, and draw the next section of wall. This section will be slightly larger if it is projected forward and slightly smaller if it is projected backward. This change in size, however, may be estimated because it is so slight. Continue making these adjustments until all of the major surfaces have been moved and sketched in place.

5. Trace or draw the detail elements in the drawing, including the details that might appear on the foreshortened walls. Figures 3-2a and 3-2b

show the adjustments which can be made to an elevated drawing, with the details drawn in at the last step. Most of these details can be traced from the original elevation as the change in scale on the moved sections of the drawing is very slight. Round elements in the interior elevation, such as a column, are indicated by a straight line in the elevation, when enhancing that elevation to a shallow perspective, those lines should be slightly curved to suggest their roundness.

6. Once the construction of the new perspective and elevation is complete, another overlay should be made and a tracing done to fix a desirable composition and a consistent line quality.

EXAGGERATED LINE WEIGHT

Line weights were discussed in Chapter 2 as a way of enhancing perspective drawings, but note that exaggerated line weights also can be used to enhance a flat-parallel line drawing. The lines used to draw an elevation usually represent the edges of surfaces, and these edges can be thought of as facing either left, right, up, or down. By assigning line weight to these edges, depending upon which way they face, the viewer is reminded that these lines represent edges on three-dimensional surfaces; Hence the viewer will more easily understand the elevation as having some depth. See the sketch of a nurse's station in Figures 3-3a and 3-3b for an example of the way in which a viewer's understanding is enhanced with the following techniques. To assign line weight, one could think of the subject of the elevation as being illuminated by a strong light source from either the top left or right. As such, the edges facing the light source will be highlighted, and those facing away from the light source will be shaded. The highlighted edges then will be drawn with a light line and the shade edges with a heavy line. To implement this technique assign a light weight to all the lines representing the edges that face left or the top of the drawing, a medium weight to lines for edges that face down, and a heavy weight to lines for edges that face right. The edges that would be highlighted strongly by the light source can be drawn by two thin parallel lines leaving a thin white space between the lines. The visual effect of this convention upon the viewer is that of a bright highlight. Another useful convention to exaggerate line weight in an elevation drawing is to offset horizontal and vertical lines slightly when surfaces change. For example, when a wall section is further

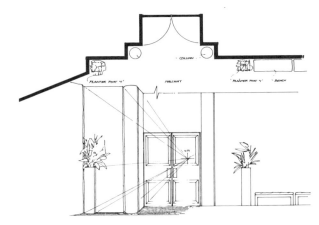

Figure 3–2a
The right-hand side of this drawing is a standard elevation; the left-hand side has been adjusted to indicate shallow depth. Carpet has been added to suggest the floor plane.

Figure 3–2b
Once an elevation has been adjusted to show shallow depth, details can be sketched in, or decorative variations can be tried. A final tracing from this drawing would be made for presentation.

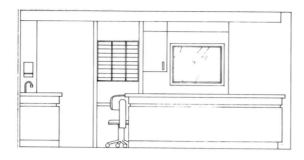

Figure 3–3a
Elevation drawing of a nurses station using a single-line weight. Drawings such as this are not as easily understood as ones with enhanced-line work.

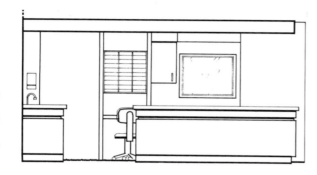

Figure 3–3b
The same elevation as Figure 3-3a; however, the line weights have been enhanced and their positions adjusted slightly to help the viewer to understand the space.

Figure 3–4
This elevation of a boot display illustrates how a shadow can help describe the shape of a triangular shelf that would otherwise not be understood in an elevation drawing.

back in space than one adjacent to it, the designer can drop the line that describes the top edge slightly and raise the line that describes the bottom edge. These are very subtle changes, but they will give the viewer a cue to the wall sections as being in different spatial planes. This offsetting of lines can be done with detail elements also, such as furniture legs and freestanding objects shown in the elevation.

SHADE AND SHADOW

The use of a strong light source to help enhance an elevation or a plan drawing can be taken further and with more dramatic effect than modifying line weights. Shadows, shaded areas, and highlights can be drawn into a parallel-line drawing with very good results. Shadows have the strongest impact as they help the viewer to see depth changes in a drawing. An object that casts a shadow upon a wall will be seen as one that comes forward in the pictorial space, and the shape of the shadow will help the viewer to understand the shape of the object. For example, a triangular shelf on a wall drawn in elevation gives no clue to its triangular shape; however, the shadow will be triangular and thus clue the viewer as to the shape of the shell. Shadows also add contrast to drawings; where a light surface is contrasted by a darker shadow, the lighter surface tends to move forward in the picture plane. See how the use of shadow is used in the display in Figure 3-4. Because all the lines in an elevation are parallel, it is considerably easier to project shadows on an elevation than to project shadows in a perspective drawing.

To plan a shadow on an elevation, the designer first draws a diagonal line through the corner of the object casting the shadow; this represents the light ray from an assigned light source. Next he or she determines how long the shadow is to be and marks that distance on the light ray. This should be done for all forward corners of the object casting the shadow, and then these marks are connected. The designer draws a line back to the point where the object touches the wall, and fills the shadow in with a light- or mid-gray value (Fig. 3-5). Where shadows fall over irregular surfaces, those portions which are forward in the picture plane will have the shadows cast on them shorten, and those surfaces that recede from the picture plane will have longer shadows cast on them. This technique of adding shadows to elevations can be done at almost any level of drawing, from very tight mechanical elevations to loose freehand sketches of elevations.

In addition to adding shadows, shaded areas can be added to elevation drawings. If both shadows and shaded areas are going to be used, it is a good idea to make the shadows slightly darker than the shaded areas to aid the visual reading of the drawing and to distinguish between surfaces.

A shade surface is one that does not receive direct light from the light source and does not have a shadow cast over it. Typically there are not many shade surfaces visible in an elevation or plan drawing, although Figure 3-6 shows how they can be added. They are common in isometric drawings however. In an elevation, surfaces which are not parallel or perpendicular to the picture plane may show a shade side, and curved surfaces likely will show a shade side. These surfaces can be tinted a light-gray value which will distinguish them from shadows and surfaces lit directly by the light source. In some instances, particularly in loose or freehand orthographic sketches, shading can be sketched in to suggest depth or portions of surfaces which are furthest from the light source. In an elevation drawing where one section of the wall is back from the picture plane, that far wall may be shaded a very light gray. The end furthest from the light source on a large expanse of wall may be shaded lightly. One side of the floor surface on floor plans may be shaded, or lower levels may be rendered a light gray to show their depth.

Finally, highlights may be added to elevations and other drawings in essentially the same manner as mentioned in the section on line weights. Two thin parallel lines will create a highlight edge or, in some instances, a broken line or lines may be used.

RENDERED SURFACES

Perspective rendering will be discussed fully in Chapter 5. There are, however, some basic rendering conventions that are useful for enhancing orthographic drawings. These conventions also relate to an assigned light source in the drawing.

When rendering objects, it is customary to contrast one surface with another. For instance, the top surface of a cube may be rendered in a light value to show that it faces the light source; that surface then will be contrasted against a darker-side surface which receives less illumination from the light source. The contrasting of surfaces, as shown in the illustration in

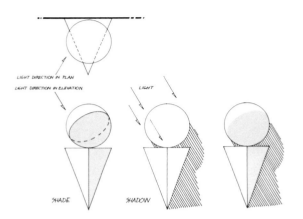

Figure 3-5
Shade and shadow are added to this elevation of a wall detail. The direction of light in both plan and elevation views is considered when planning the shade and shadow areas.

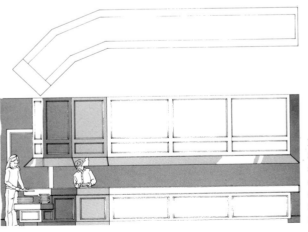

Figure 3-6
Shaded areas have been added to this elevation view of a food-service line. Light enters from the left, putting the back wall and angled surfaces in shade.

Figure 3-7, helps the viewer to see the cube as a three-dimensional object.

In an elevation drawing, only one surface of any object is shown; therefore, to develop the contrast needed to enhance the perception of three-dimensional space, the flat surfaces must be rendered to show the effects of light washing across them. When light strikes a flat surface such as a wall, the portion of the surface closest to the light is brightest, and the portion furthest from the light source is darkest. This provides us with a workable convention in rendering elevations as all flat surfaces will have three values: a light-highlight area, a middle-value area over most of the surface, and a darker-value area furthest from the assigned light source. This range of values may be very narrow, as in all light gray values, or the range of values may be great for a dramatic, exaggerated effect. When selecting the gray range to use on a surface, a good rule to remember is that light-colored surfaces use a range of light grays, and dark-colored surfaces use a range of dark grays. If there is a selection of gray markers ranging from 1 to 10, where 1 is 10 percent black and 10 is 100 percent or pure black, a white wall might be rendered with the numbers-1- and 2-gray markers. The white of the paper will serve as the highlight ares. It is possible to render the white wall with only a number-1-gray marker, double-coating the paper where the darkest value is to go. To render a dark wall, numbers-4, 5, and 6 gray might be used, rendering the first quarter of the surface with a 40 percent gray, the middle half of the surface a 50 percent gray, and the final quarter of the surface the darkest value, a 60 percent gray. By deciding the relative value of surfaces in the elevation, a light wall, a dark door, and

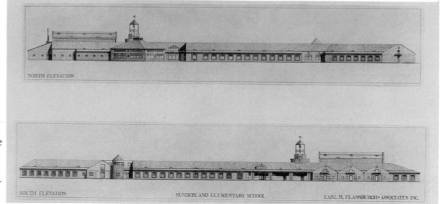

Figure 3–7
A rendered elevation such as this greatly enhances the viewer's understanding of the space. This drawing was done in colored pencil and ink. *Earl R. Flansburgh + Associates, Inc., Boston, MA.*

such, and then rendering them with modulated values, the elevation picks up contrast both among individual surfaces and between one surface to another. The drawing takes on added interest and is easier for the viewer to visualize it as three-dimensional space.

AUXILIARY DRAWINGS

To help the viewer understand plan and elevation drawings, the addition of auxiliary drawings may be the simplest and most effective way for the designer to explain the interior space. An elevation drawing with a plan view of that elevation directly above it will give the experienced viewer enough information to construct a mental perspective of that space. Plan drawings are often enhanced by showing a section-view through the space and adding drawings of the most important elevations. These auxiliary drawings should be positioned close to the main drawing, and line work in each should correspond directly. Figures 3-8a and 3-8b demonstrate how the auxiliary drawing is used to support the plan drawing.

Other types of auxiliary drawings are sketches showing significant details of the interior (Figs. 3-9a and 3-9b). A perspective sketch or an enhanced elevation showing the focal point of a large, complex elevation may be enough to suggest the design character of that interior to the viewer.

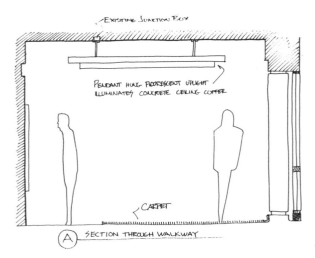

Figure 3–8b
Section view of a hallway. These two drawings illustrate how an auxiliary-section view can aid the understanding of a plan drawing. *PHH Avenue, Chicago, IL.*

Figure 3–8a
Plan view of a hallway. *PHH Avenue, Chicago, IL.*

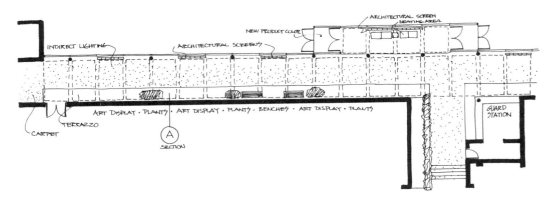

Floor plans can be made more meaningful by including sketches of the major components of that interior. These sketches should be keyed to the floor plan and presented in close proximity to the plan, as the intent is to let the viewer create a mental perspective of the interior.

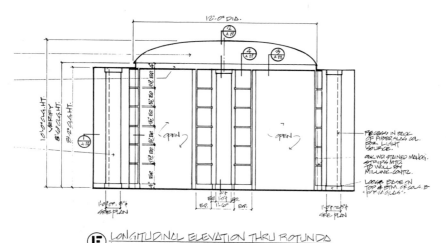

Figure 3–9a
Elevation through a rotunda.
Paul B. Berger and Associates, Chicago, IL.

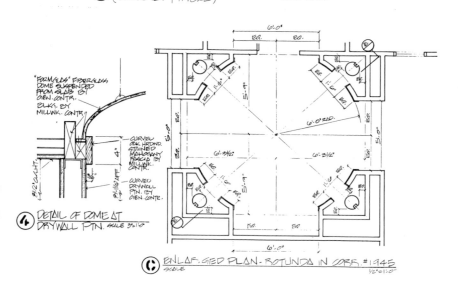

Figure 3–9b
Plan view of a rotunda. These two drawings complement each other providing detailed information about an architectural feature of an interior. *Paul B. Berger and Associates, Chicago, IL.*

4

Compositional Elements of Perspective

Perspective is a technique of representing three-dimensional space and objects on a two-dimensional surface, creating the illusion of volume and space. Because perspective drawing is seen as the most realistic representation of an interior, it is often the centerpiece of a design presentation. Since perspective-line drawing provides the basic structure for an interior-color sketch or rendering, it therefore, must be accurate. Otherwise the resulting drawing will look awkward and will interfere with the viewer's understanding of the design content of the drawing.

This shows the importance of having a good working knowledge both of perspective and of the conventions for drawing in perspective. A working knowledge will enable a designer to become more comfortable with perspective sketching, enabling him or her to achieve a quick, easy look to the work and allow him or her to work faster and with greater control over the perspective composition. A variety of other texts do an excellent job of explaining the theory and mechanics of perspective drawing; several of these dealing with interiors are listed in the bibliography. The discussion of perspective in this text will focus on quick methods of perspective construction and control, of both the composition and the choice of view in perspective drawing.

Figure 4–1
The vanishing point in this one-point perspective is to the far left within the picture plane, suggesting an almost two-point perspective view of the interior. Aircraft interior. *Walter Dorwin Teague Associates, New York, NY.*

Figure 4–2
This is a typical one-point perspective, showing a room with one wall removed. Elevator lobby. *PHH Avenue, Chicago, IL.*

One- and two-point perspective are the two most common techniques used for drawing interiors. The major difference between them is how objects are presented in the drawing. In one-point perspective, examples of which are shown in Figures 4-1 and 4-2, one wall of a room is removed; the viewer looks into the room directly at the opposing wall, and the two side walls can be seen either partially or in total depending upon the composition. In two-point perspective (Fig. 4-3), the view into the room is oblique to the rear wall, two walls of the room are visible, and most of the floor plan can be included if desired. The choice of which system to use will depend as much on the shape of the interior as what is to be shown. While one-point perspective may be faster and simpler to construct, the drawing has a stage-like quality because the viewer is confronted by the flat back wall and, usually, the full front or side of the furnishings. There is little sense of the viewer's being brought into the interior. However for interiors with deep space, such as a hallway, where the wall treatment is important or where walls are not at right angles to each other, one-point perspective may be the preferred view. Figure 4-4 depicts such an effective use of one-point perspective.

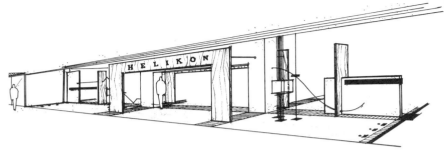

Figure 4-3
This is a hallway drawn in two-point perspective. Rather than looking down the hall as is common with a one-point perspective view, this drawing shows more of the office front. Helikon project. *Eva Maddox Associates, Chicago, IL.*

Figure 4-4
This is a photograph of the finished Helikon office. The photograph is essentially a one-point-perspective view. Helikon project. *Eva Maddox Associates, Chicago, IL. Nick Merrick photographer.*

Figure 4–5
Two-point perspective was used in this drawing to give a good visual impression of the volumetric space of the climbing structure in the center of the drawing. Park School of Brookline project. *Earl R. Flansburgh + Associates;* Interior recreation space. *Donald A. Reed.*

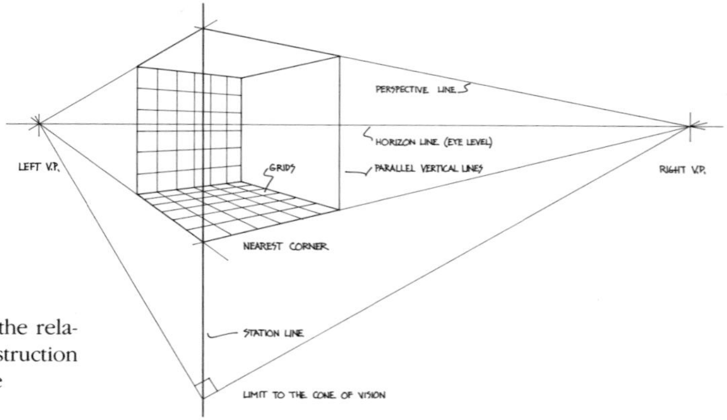

Figure 4–6
This diagram shows the relative locations of construction lines in a perspective drawing.

Two-point perspective may be considered more effective because it presents a more open view of an interior. The construction lines converge to the vanishing points and open up toward the viewer to create a more dynamic, visual feeling. Objects in the interior usually are presented obliquely to the line of sight, making them more active and interesting to view. Two-point perspective can effectively show furniture groupings, typically square or near-square rooms and constructions of special interest in an interior, as are shown in Figures 4-5 and 4-6.

The following is a list of terms and principles of perspective essential to an understanding of perspective-sketching techniques.

▶ Perspective lines are lines in an interior that move away from the viewer and converge to a vanishing point. Vanishing points are located on the horizon line.

▶ The horizon line runs horizontally through the drawing to represent the eye level of the viewer. When setting up a perspective-construction system, place the horizon line at the height and scale the room is to be viewed. It should be above the drawing for a bird's-eye view, and at just over 5 feet in scale above the ground line for a standing adult.

▶ A station line runs perpendicular to the horizon line. This line indicates the viewer's line of sight and should be positioned carefully to determine the vantage point a viewer will have when looking into the room. Figures 4-7a and 4-7b demonstrate the significance of the perspective view chosen to illustrate an interior.

▶ In two-point perspective, the corner of the room closest to the viewer (at the bottom of the drawing) should be greater than 90 degrees. If it is less than that, the drawing will look distorted.

▶ All vertical lines in a drawing are parallel to each other and are perpendicular to the horizon line and ground line. Note that in a photograph of an interior, these lines converge, and, when drawing from a photograph, the vertical lines need to be corrected so that they are perpendicular to the ground.

▶ A floor grid or wall grid is a perspective-drawing technique for dividing up a surface into square units, in perspective. These guides allow the designer to locate quickly the correct placement of objects in the interior drawing.

WORKING IN PERSPECTIVE

The following discussion should help designers control the perspective layout of an interior as well as assist in planning an effective composition for the drawing.

Choice of Interior View

Choosing a perspective view of an interior requires the designer to visualize the interior from a number of different vantage points and to select one that shows the points of interest in the interior to their best advantage. Two things will aid the designer in this choice. First the designer should have a good idea of what the drawing is to be used for, and what he or she wants to show with this perspective. Second, the designer must have a complete floor plan on which a station line can be drawn to show the line of sight looking into the room. Typically the line of sight should be unobstructed as it enters the room, and the major focal point of the interior should be close to this line. The designer also will want to choose a point of view that is not through the center of the room. By having the view off to one side, there is a dynamic balance in the composition that adds interest to the drawing.

Once it is known what to show in a drawing and from what viewpoint it will be seen, some quick thumbnail sketches can be made to determine the horizon line (eye level), plan the composition, and serve as a guide for setting up the proper perspective system. One of the most frustrating occurrences in perspective drawing is to set up a perspective system and find out that the interior it produces is too small and from a poor viewpoint, or that it does not show the design features well. To avoid this, some designers adapt a few "stock" perspective layouts and choose from among them for each drawing situation. Another potential solution is to determine the perspective-construction layout from sketches as outlined in the following procedure.

1. Using a freehand or triangle-assisted sketching technique, redraw the thumbnail sketch that best represents the interior. When working in two-point perspective, draw the further corner of the room and the floor area. Imagine that the back walls are there and sketch in the interior furnishings and other elements. If the floor area is the wrong size, it can be enlarged or reduced easily to come into scale with the inte-

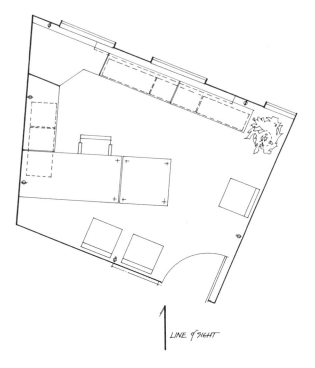

Figure 4–7a
An appropriate view of an interior should be selected to show the design features. In this project the desk-furniture system was the focus.

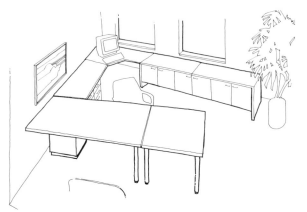

Figure 4–7b
This drawing is a perspective view of the sight line shown in Figure 4-7a.

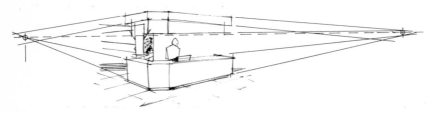

Figure 4-8a
To set up a perspective, first sketch the interior as you want to present it. Then project the perspective lines to find the vanishing points. Be sure to locate the vanishing points on a level horizon line.

Figure 4-8b
With vanishing points established, redraw the organized sketch to correct inaccurate perspective lines and adjust all vertical lines so they are parallel to each other.

rior elements. Once the interior is roughed out, draw in the top edge of the back walls and any wall or ceiling treatment, as has been done in Figure 4-8a.

2. This will give a very rough interior sketch. The important aspects are that it is the size that is wanted and the viewpoint best suited to the design features. Now tape down the drawing so the station line is perpendicular to the table edge. With a T square running along the table edge, adjust the major vertical lines in the drawing so they are parallel to the station line (Fig. 4-8b). A colored pencil may be used for this so the lines are not lost in the sketch lines.

3. With a long, straightedge extend the perspective lines until they converge to the vanishing points on the right and left sides of the drawing. The vanishing points probably will not be level and should be moved so they are on a horizontal line. If one of the vanishing points is too far from the drawing to use conveniently, it should be moved in along the horizon line. Note that if it is moved very much, the drawing should be shifted approximately one half the distance that the vanishing point was moved, and in the same direction.

4. Once the drawing has a fixed-horizon line, vanishing points, and station line, redraw with a bold black pen the major perspective lines and vertical edges in the room. This is the perspective layout that can be fit into a construction system to produce the desired size, view, and composition for the drawing. Figure 4-8c shows how the addition of these details completes the sketch.

Composition

With the point of view chosen and the perspective layout made, the composition of the drawing becomes important. In order to bring the viewer into the drawing, furnishings can be positioned in the foreground so the viewer looks in over them. Such a device is shown in Figure 4-9. Showing the stop edge of a chair or the corner of a table in the foreground and fading out that piece of furniture towards the edge of the paper will not only let the viewer "feel" in the room but will also bring some of the white of the paper into the drawing to suggest that the room continues beyond the page and around the viewer. In a similar fashion, the entire drawing can fade into the paper at the edges. This not only becomes more inviting for the viewer, but it again brings the white of the paper into the drawing to thereby add a sense of light and liveliness to the drawing and reduce the number of square inches of paper that needs drawing attention; thus saving time. Another compositional device is to leave at least a 2-inch border of paper around the drawing. This will keep the drawing from looking crowded on the page and offer an opportunity for a title block, or other identification, and a border. The title block serves as a solid base for a drawing and provides information that relates the drawing to the rest of the presentation. A thin-border line around the drawing offers an opportunity to dramatize the perspective. By breaking the border with the major perspective lines, the room appears to be moving beyond the picture frame and around the viewer.

Focus

Any single drawing can serve only a limited role in communicating design information. Rather than trying to show all in a perspective drawing, it is more effective and realistic to highlight or to focus on specific design information. This can be anything from the architectural treatment of the room and color scheme to the use of furniture in the interior. The crucial thing is to know what to show and to compose the drawing with the focus to the center of the page and, as mentioned before, to use an off-center view through the room to the focal point. The focal point will be delineated and, perhaps, rendered with the most attention, detail, and contrast. This drawing attention will fade towards the edges of the paper to reinforce the focus of the drawing.

Atmosphere

The designer's achievement of a sense of atmosphere in an interior rendering is probably the most difficult and intangible aspect of drawing. Atmosphere conveys the feeling that there is air and light in the space, which thus suggests that the drawing represents a potentially real space. The drawing is not photorealistic, but it has a lively quality to it. The primary element that adds to atmosphere in an interior drawing is light. While light itself

Figure 4-8c
With the adjusted-perspective sketch, add details until the line drawing is complete and ready to be used as an underlay for a rendering.

Figure 4-9
This perspective sketch fades towards the edges of the composition, which focuses the viewer's attention on the center of the drawing.

Figure 4-10
Shade and shadows are
important in a drawing to
convey a sense of light. In
this sketch the shade and
shadow areas are casually put
in to suggest the light from
the windows along the
hallway.

cannot be drawn, it can be suggested through the use of shade, shadow, contrast, unrendered paper, line weight, color values, and reflection.

▶ Shade and shadows can be plotted along with the perspective construction of the interior once the various light sources have been determined. As a pictorial device, however, shadows can be manipulated to enhance the focus of a drawing. Toward the center of the page, shadows and shade surfaces are darker in order to build contrast with the light surfaces and are generally softer towards the edges of the composition. Figure 4-10 demonstrates the use of shade and shadow to suggest incoming sunlight. Shadows and shade surfaces also can be used to silhouette small objects or parts of furniture or to show the topography or texture of the surfaces these objects are adjacent to, or fall across. When sketching a shadow or a shade surface, render the darkest portion at the base, and lighten the surface or shadow as it moves away from the base. This shows the tendency for shadows to lighten upwards due to reflected light from objects and wall surfaces.

▶ Contrast is a relative quality in a drawing and is usually underplayed. High contrast is achieved by putting light and dark shades adjacent to each other in a drawing; low contrasts are a result of gradual changes from light to dark shades (Fig. 4-11). Even in a pencil drawing when all the values are fairly light, a high contrast can be built if the designer utilizes the values available.

The first step in using contrast in a drawing is to establish the value keys for the drawing. This is simply done by drawing in the darkest and lightest surfaces in the composition. If the lightest surface is the white of the paper, then what is left to determine is the darkest value. Generally line work will be black, but, if large areas of black are not going to be used, the black line should not be considered the darkest value. Shading may be done with parallel-line work, to give an overall gray which may be the darkest value. Once value keys are established, the contrasts of the focal point of the drawing can be planned; the focal point is usually the area of highest contrast in the drawing. From this point, move towards the edges of the page and lower the contrast as the eye moves out from the center of the page.

▶ Paper value refers to the color of the paper and how it is used in the drawing. White paper is what makes colored markers, chalk, and transparent watercolors glow on the page. The white paper is said to be the light in the drawing. By allowing paper to show through in the drawing, the quality of light is reinforced. Drawings where 100 percent of the surface is covered with value or color can look muddy and dull. White paint often must be added to bring back the light, but this may make the drawing look overworked. Opaque rendering materials, such as designer's gauche, are intended for total coverage, but these materials are meant for complex-color renderings. As the amount of drawing involvement diminishes towards the edge of the page, more light is seen to be flooding onto the room. This supports the relatively small amount of paper showing through the rendered area at the focal point. If an interior should seem dark, just darken the paper at the edges of the drawing, a technique similar to drawing on black paper.

▶ Line quality was discussed previously in reference to light and contrast, but is also important to the rendering of interiors. A line drawing can use different line weights to describe edges; it can utilize a series of parallel lines to show value; and it can rely on lines to show texture, reflections, and pattern. These drawings usually employ only a limited amount of color: local color or flat color. The drawing depends upon line for structure and readability. As color is used more extensively in a drawing, less and less line work is employed. And in a full-scale color rendering, almost no line work is used.

Line work really does not exist in an interior. Edges are seen because of the contrast of one surface against another. But there is a tendency to overdo line in a drawing, and when lines can be left out and value or color surfaces used to describe an edge, the drawing picks up in interest.

▶ Changing the color value in a drawing is a way of modulating surfaces to suggest the wash of light across them. When using a colored pencil, a gradation can be drawn from light to dark. While the color has not changed, there is a value change in the color from a pale value to the full, intense color. Draw the dark or shade value of that color by blending it with its complementary color, or with a gray, to result in a slightly duller value. When using markers to add color to a drawing, it is necessary to have a series of markers in each color to form a value pallet. A typical value pallet would consist of five markers ranging from a very light, pale value of the color, say, for example, ice blue, to a

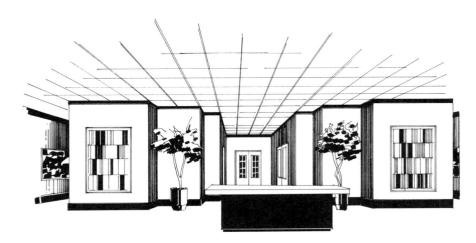

Figure 4–11
The contrast in this drawing has been exaggerated to illustrate how dramatically light and dark surfaces can be contrasted.

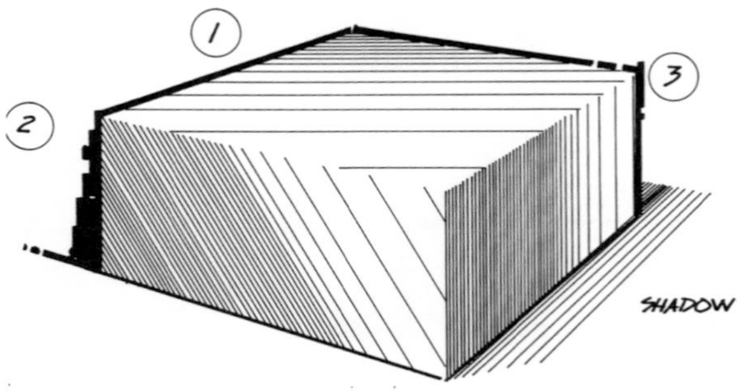

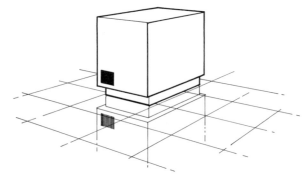

Figure 4–12
Each side of an object to be rendered has a different value range, graded from light to dark. Even the shadow lightens as it moves away from the object.

SHADOW

Figure 4–13
A reflection can be suggested with vertical strokes down from the object into the floor surface. The reflection is usually lighter than the object itself.

deep, very dark value, such as prussian blue. The number-3 marker in that series would be a clear, bright blue. When applying the colors to the surfaces in the drawing, keep the surfaces that face the light source the lightest value, and make the surfaces that are in the shade a darker value. Also, each surface should be modulated from a light to a dark value within the relative value assigned for that surface. These gradations of shade are illustrated in Figure 4-12. It is helpful to think of the rule of three, three values per object: top, front, and shade sides; and three values per surface: the highlight area, the true color area, and the slightly shaded area. In so doing, objects thus will appear to be bathed in light.

Reflections are used only occasionally in interior sketches, and when they are, it is done usually with only a quick, short-hand gesture technique as in the quick, vertical strokes used in Figure 4-13. More complex reflections are commonly used in product rendering and illustration. A reflection may be characterized as a pale mirror image of an object shown in another surface. In perspective drawing, the object and the distance the object is from the reflective surface both are reflected, and the height of the object and its distance from the reflective surface, if any, is the same perspective measure as the reflection. Since most reflections in interiors are from vertical objects on flat surfaces, a convention of using a quick, vertical stroke can be used to show reflections on floors and tables. This can be done with a line or with a broad, light-value market stroke.

Special Perspective Problems

One of the most difficult aspects of perspective is the drawing of circular objects, particularly a circle in perspective, an ellipse. There are guides to help draw accurate ellipses and, one needs to know which ellipse to select and how to position it. If using a perspective system, the ellipse can be drawn by filling a square with an ellipse. If the designer is at a freehand stage of drawing, the following steps will help him or her to select and position an ellipse.

An ellipse has a major and a minor axis that are always perpendicular to each other and run through the center of the ellipse, as shown in Figure 4-14. When drawing a cylinder, the minor or short axis of the ellipse can be thought of as running through the length of the cylinder, and the major or long axis is perpendicular to the minor axis and should be drawn at the ends of the cylinder. With the two axes drawn, the width of the cylinder should be marked along the major axis with the minor axis at the center point; these form end points of the major axis. An ellipse now can be drawn between those end points along the major axis. The thickness or roundness of the ellipse still must be determined, a task aided greatly by an experienced eye (Fig. 4-15). Draw a perspective line from both vanishing points through the end point of the major axis. The points where these perspective lines meet are also points on the ellipse. With four points now determined, an ellipse can be drawn in either freehand or with the use of an ellipse guide. To check the accuracy of an ellipse, draw a line from a vanishing point through a section of the ellipse; the section of that line inside the ellipse should be bisected equally by another line drawn through the center of the ellipse to the other vanishing point.

In any situation where a circle needs to be drawn in perspective, the circle should be thought of as the end of a cylinder with the minor axis going through the length of the cylinder, and with the major axis perpendicular to the minor axis. This will ensure that all the ellipses are positioned correctly in the drawing.

The use of overlays when setting up a perspective sketch is a technique which allows a great deal of experimentation with the pictorial space. On the first sheet of paper, the basic mechanical perspective is drawn to set up the interior and the major interior elements, often as perspective blocks without details. This sheet also has the floor and wall grids which aid the quick placement of details in the interior. If there are many construction lines on the drawing, the designer should darken the important perspective lines and, if necessary, use colored pencils to distinguish one set of line work from another. Using an overlay sheet of semitransparent paper, the designer can trace the interior and add more detail to the drawing. Continuing this process of overlays, the interior composition is complete. The complete line drawing on tracing paper now can be reproduced to opaque paper with copy machines or traced onto drawing paper using a light table. During the tracing, ideas for the placement of furniture or architectural changes in the interior can be sketched on overlays and made part of the drawing, or the sheet can be pulled and other ideas tried. In a like manner, he or

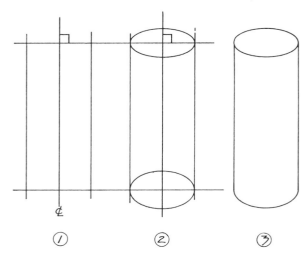

Figure 4-14
To correctly position an ellipse, it should be thought of as the end of a cylinder with the minor axis running the length of the imagined cylinder.

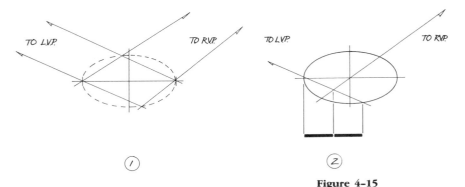

Figure 4-15
The roundness of an ellipse can be determined by drawing perspective lines through the end points of the desired ellipses major axis. The points where the perspective lines cross will be on the ellipse.

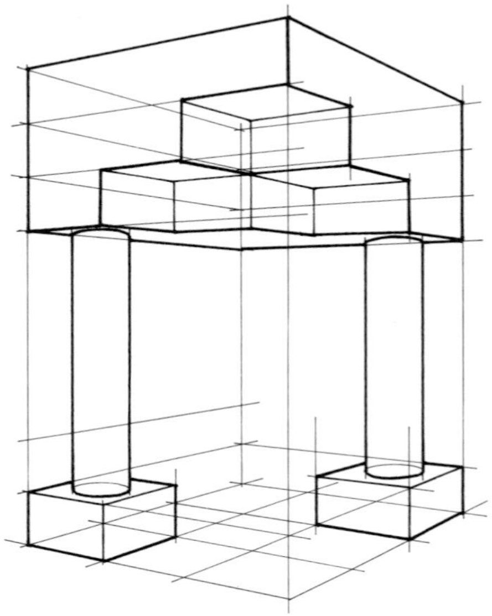

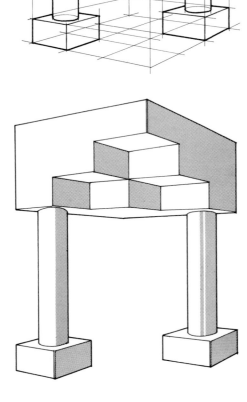

Figure 4–16a
By subdividing a box in perspective, objects can be "carved" by removing portions of the perspective volume.

Figure 4–16b
Once the perspective lines are removed, the "carved" object is easily understood. Using tracing overlays, additional detail can be added to this block drawing.

she can experiment with drawing; shadows or wall contrasts can be visualized or traced and then incorporated or rejected.

When drawing furniture and other objects in an interior, a technique of perspective-box construction is efficient and fast. The basic premise is to see the object fit into a series of geometric boxes, a process illustrated in Figure 4-16a. The box or boxes are drawn into the perspective layout to position the item, then the designer begins to cut away at these boxes and add details until the desired form is revealed. The progressive refinement of the form largely will be done freehand, sometimes using a triangle as a straight-edge to keep the lines crisp.

There are times when one will want to build with box units rather than cut away at one large box. To do this, construct the initial box, which does not have to be a cube, and visualize putting another identical box next to it in perspective. The following steps will help to make this clear in the drawing.

1. Draw diagonal lines through the corners of one side of the first box.

2. Draw a perspective line through the center point of that side of the box through the vertical edges of that side.

3. Draw another diagonal line from the top front corner of that side of the box through the midpoint of the back edge of that side. Continue the line until it intersects the perspective line used to create the bottom edge of the initial box. In Figure 4-16b, the revealed object is ready for additional detail.

4. That new point is one box length back in perspective from the initial box. Draw a vertical rule from that point to the perspective line used to construct the top edge of the initial box. This forms the back edge of the new box. The rest of the new box can be constructed with standard perspective techniques (Fig. 4-17a, 4-17b, and 4-17c).

By either carving or multiplying boxes, almost any object in the interior can be positioned and drawn without an excessive amount of perspective construction involving vanishing points and measuring lines.

One final shortcut to perspective drawing involves a rough cardboard model of the interior space. Spray mount a print of the floor plan to a piece of foam-core board and, on this floor plan, position vertical walls by hot gluing precut-foam-core wall sections. If there are elevation drawings, spray mount these to the appropriate walls. Position small blocks of wood on the floor plan to show furniture. While this model may be developed into a presentable space model, it may remain simply a very rough, disposable sketch model. View the model through a hole in a piece of cardboard to choose a perspective view for the interior drawing. Then photograph the model from that view using a macro lens on the camera to keep as much of the model in focus as possible. From an enlarged photograph, which can be made by projecting and tracing it or by developing it in the darkroom, the vanishing points can be located and the interior elements positioned by projecting lines up from the floor plan and out from the wall elevations. It is helpful when using this technique to include a floor and wall grid or other scale indicators on the floor plan and elevations.

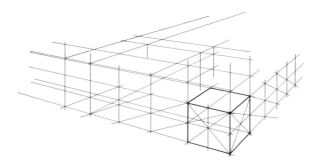

Figure 4-17a
An initial box can be multiplied in perspective to build a perspective volume.

Figure 4-17c
Details may be added until a believable space is created around the object.

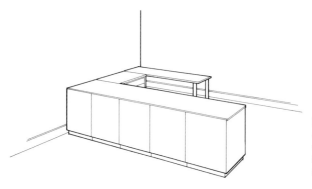

Figure 4-17b
A tracing of the perspective volume is made to bring out the object lines describing this desk system.

5
Basic Rendering Conventions

Most interiors are made up of typical elements that could be classified either as floor coverings, furniture, wall treatments, ceiling systems, or such. When making a perspective rendering of an interior, standard rendering conventions are used to indicate these typical elements in an interior. The process of making a rendering or a presentation sketch of an interior can be thought of as using a series of rendering conventions for each of the elements in the interior. The final appearance and style of the drawings are determined by the particular way these rendering conventions are used by the designer.

This chapter discusses how light and color determine the rendering of elements and offers suggestions for working with color.

BASICS OF COLOR AND LIGHT

The aim of color in an interior rendering is to offer as much richness and color information as possible. However, working with color can be confusing because light color, shade, shadow, light intensity, surface texture, and material all affect the local color (actual color) of the object.

To complicate color work further, art materials come in a wealth of colors with no apparent system for their selection or use in an interior rendering. In order to make sense of this, it will help to review some color terms.

There are three aspects to any one color which should be understood in order to select colors for rendering. They are hue, value, and intensity.

Hue. Hue is the name of a color: Red, for example, is a hue. Any particular hue may vary in both value and intensity. Pink is actually a light value of red, and burgundy is a dark value of red. Hues are often arranged on a color wheel which help designers to understand the mixing of colors. There are three primary hues: yellow, red, and blue; and all other hues are mixtures of those primaries. Red and yellow together make orange; red and blue together make violet; and yellow and blue together make green. Hues across from each other on the color wheel are called complements and, when mixed, produce a neutral brown or gray. Figure 5-1 shows the color wheel and gray scale which assist the designer in his or her selection of color.

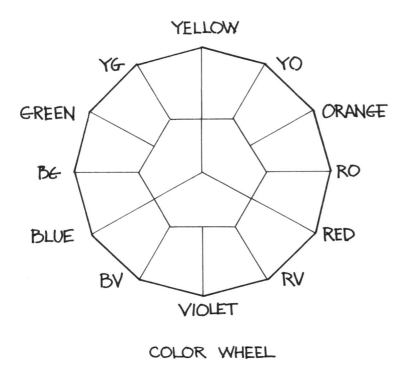

COLOR WHEEL

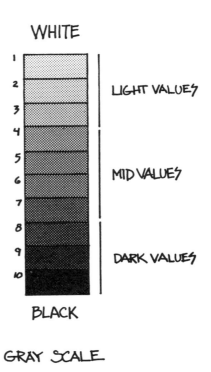

GRAY SCALE

Figure 5-1
Color wheel and gray scale showing the relative location of colors and gray values to each other.

There are many systems for naming colors, from numbers to common names. The traditional color wheel uses compound names to identify colors. For example, colors ranging from red to orange would be red (R), red red-orange (RRO), red-orange (RO), orange red-orange (ORO), and orange (O). As can be seen, the distinctions between hues can be great, as between red and green, or very subtle, as between red and red red-orange. Therefore, when selecting a series of colors of one hue such as red, one must be careful not to confuse red orange with light red. To help when selecting a specific hue, look for the amount of the adjacent primary hue on the color wheel. For example, look for the amount of yellow or the amount of blue contained in a red when selecting that hue.

Value. The value of a color refers to its lightness or darkness. Any hue can be arranged from light to dark like a series of grays. Red would range from pink through red to burgundy. A light value, called a tint, is a mixture of the hue and white. A dark value of a hue is called a shade and can be considered a mixture of that hue with black. A common mistake made when drawing with either markers, pencils, or chalk is to assume a light value of a color can be made by applying the color lightly and letting more of the white paper show, and a darker value of the color made by rubbing the tool very firmly into the paper. To a very limited extent, there will be a slight value change; more likely, however, you will get either a pale color showing the texture of the paper or a smudge of shiny color. To obtain different values of a color, you must select separate drawing tools with the proper hue and value.

Intensity. Intensity is the brightness of a color. The color wheel shows hues that are considered to be at their fullest intensity, while for each color on the color wheel, there are versions which are less intense or dull. For example, a bright green, perhaps called grass green, is a fully intense color. An olive drab may be the same hue as the grass green, only less intense. Since less-intense colors are dull and more neutral, they are important to designers in helping control the visual dominance of elements. When selecting colors with which to render, include the less-intense colors and also, get different values for the less-intense colors, as for example, a pale olive drab and a deep olive drab.

Before a discussion of the selection of colors for an interior rendering, it will help to discuss how light affects color. Any object in an interior is made visible by light reflecting off of the surface. The amount of light and how it is reflected will modify the perception of the color of that object, which means that the selections of colors for a rendering is based on how one wants to represent the light in the drawing.

As light strikes an object and is subsequently reflected, one part of the object is closest to the light source and faces it more directly than other parts. This part or side is said to be highlighted. The object also will have a moderately lit side or surface and a portion or side which is dark or in shade. Each of these different light conditions can be rendered with different values or a single hue including a tint used for the highlight side, a mid-value for the moderately lit side, and a shade value for the dark side. Therefore, drawing tools with a value range for each hue to be used are important. This includes a value range for fully intense colors like red as well as one for neutrals or low-intense colors like olive drab.

Such flat surfaces as walls also reflect different amounts of light along their length. As a wall recedes into the drawing, it will become darker, but as it moves toward the viewer or a light source, it will appear lighter. For convenience, a three-value system for rendering any object can be used, depicting a light, medium, and dark side to the objects. Coupled with this is a value system for each surface which modulates each surface from light to dark. For a light surface, a series of light values would be used. A white wall, for example, might be rendered with number-1 and number-2 warm-gray markers.

SELECTING A COLOR PALETTE

A color palette for rendering consists of individual color groups of drawing tools. Although colored markers specifically will be discussed here, the same groupings can be made with pencils and chalks. For each hue desired in the palette, a series of three to five markers should be selected ranging from a light tint to a deep shade of that hue. If possible, the light tint should be a slightly warmer color and the shade color slightly cooler. For example, the light tint should have a hint of yellow in it and the shade marker a hint of blue in it. This represents the color of light modifying the object color. It suggests the highlight side reflects warm sunlight, and the shade side, which does not receive direct sunlight but does receive reflected blue skylight, reflects a slightly cooler color. In addition to the range of values for each hue in the palette, there are some good accent colors which add interest to an interior. For instance, a very pale light blue is used when rendering chrome, and lavender makes a good accent when used in floor reflections. Once a group of markers has been selected, number them 1, 2, 3, 4, etc., from light to dark. Now the confusion of hundreds of different-colored markers has been reduced to a few discrete groups that can be used quickly and confidently.

In addition to the colored markers, having a set of gray markers is helpful. They come in two ranges: a warm gray range which has a hint of red in it, and a cool gray range which has a hint of blue in it. Both sets are useful with the warm gray shades used for carpets, walls, and fabrics and the cool gray shades for metal and glass. It is best to have a series of ten, both warm and cool gray markers, ranging from light to dark.

With a color palette selected, make a master color-swatch sheet showing the value and hue range in the palette. This sheet, shown in Color plate 1, will serve as a guide for selecting markers when doing a rendering.

Note that markers, chalks, and colored pencils are very different materials and need to be handled differently. But they can be used together in a drawing as long as care is used in their application.

BASIC MANIPULATION OF MARKERS

Markers are all basically alike in terms of how they put down color or dye. There are a variety of point sizes, ranging from very fine to broad, and each point size can produce a variety of different marks. The most common tip is a broad, wedge-shaped tip and most marker brands have a fine point available. A designer should experiment with different markers to become familiar with the kinds of strokes that can be made. Generally, each tip can make three strokes: a thin-edge stroke, a medium-end stroke, and a broad-side stroke. In addition, a variety of dabs and dots can be made with varying pressure that will be useful for texture, materials, and details.

There are a few guidelines for stroking with markers and for creating textures. Notice when stroking with a marker that when the marker is put to the paper and picked up, it will leave blobs. Also, whenever there is an overlap of strokes, the color builds up and is deeper, which will leave streaks. These effects cannot be avoided easily, but when carefully handled the effects can add to the rendering.

The first important guideline is to always stroke from edge to edge of the area to be colored. Do not stop or start the markers in the middle of the area or go back and forth across the area, or blobs and dark streaks will occur.

The buildup at the end of each stroke can work to one's advantage as it increases the contrast for edge highlights and helps to add a gradation of color to the area. As for the streaking from overlapping strokes, the streaks help the viewer to read the surface. For example, if a designer wants to emphasize the vertical qualities of a door, the markers should be stroked vertically. As one becomes more familiar with handling markers, he or she will find the stroke can convey the nature of the material. For instance, a highly reflective surface is enhanced with vertical strokes and a pooling of color at the edges. This pooling is created at the end of a stroke by pausing a moment before lifting the marker and leaving a blob of color.

If the streaking caused by overlapping marker strokes is annoying, or if the designer prefers a smooth blending of the marker color, there are two ways to eliminate streaks. The first technique is to use a nonabsorbent paper such as vellum, and blend the light and dark markers on the surface before they have time to dry. First apply the light marker over the surface. Then working quickly before the marker color dries, the darker markers are applied over the surface where they are wanted. Again, working quickly, the designer applies the light marker and blends out the streaks. It requires fast work and can be sloppy, although the designer can mask off the area with a low-tack transparent tape to ensure crisp edges.

The second method of avoiding marker streaks is to use an absorbent layout paper. This paper bleeds enough to cause the overlapping strokes to blend together. The obvious shortcoming of this method is that the bleeding which occurs at the edges of a color area requires some heavy, dark line work to crisp up these edges.

Textures can be created very directly with a marker by dabbing the marker on the paper. Carpet, for example, can be created by stippling the area; or leaves on plants can be made with a series of short, jab-like strokes. When drawing a texture, at least three markers are needed to show the lights, darks, and color changes. Before rendering a texture, the surface should be examined carefully for the following:

▶ How much light is falling on the surface? Locate the light and dark areas and where any shadows may fall across the surface.

▶ What are the basic colors that make up the surface? Be aware that overlapping the markers will create mixed colors. Have a tint and shade for each color to be used.

▶ What is the texture pattern of the surface? Choose a marker stroke to simulate the desired texture and determine a sequence of applications to simulate the pattern. Carefully plan the area for marker application. Put down the light values first, then work to the dark.

▶ Is there a color change due to a printed pattern or material change? If so, change the color of the markers used in that area. It will help to have light pencil lines drawn in as reminders where to change colors or values.

CHALK APPLICATION

Chalk and pastels have a limited use in interior renderings primarily because markers and colored pencils are much more convenient to use. There are some uses for pastels, however, that cannot be satisfied with other tools. Pastels will not adhere to hard, smooth papers like marker paper but will take nicely to toothy or soft papers like colored cover stock or diazo paper.

Chalks can be used dry or dissolved with thinner on a cotton pad. As a dry medium, the chalk can be stroked directly onto the paper from the square stock. This leaves a hard edge to the mark and is opaque to cover the marks it is drawn over. This stroke is good for highlighting, adding plant foliage, creating glare on reflective surfaces, and showing floor reflections. To tone an area, the chalk should be powdered by scraping it with a blade: Two or more colors may be powdered, picked up with a cotton pad, and rubbed onto the paper. This allows for color blending of the chalk as the designer works. An eraser will pick up the chalk and can be used to "draw" lines or to clean up edges in the chalk area.

The wet technique for applying chalk is used most commonly in backgrounds for product rendering because the effect is very bold, and is hard to control, and difficult to render details on. Simply, powdered chalk is picked up with a cotton pad, saturated with thinner, and stroked onto the paper. This method requires careful masking of the area as it is difficult to remove the chalk once applied. The following are a few guidelines for working with chalk.

► Like markers, chalks should be applied directly without repeated handling. Put a stroke down and leave it, as overworking an area makes for a smudged, muddy rendering.

► Chalks smudge easily and will melt and muddy when markers are applied over them. They also tend to clog marker tips. Therefore, put most of the chalk on a rendering at the every end, after the other work is done. Spraying fixative over chalk darkens the color slightly and, in some cases, softens the marker enough to allow it to blend with the chalk. When this occurs, the chalk color is no longer visible.

► If chalks need to be applied to marker paper, the surface must be prepared. Rubbing the paper with a fine talc, even over markers, will allow the chalks to adhere to the surface.

► To remove large amounts of chalk, blot the chalk up with a kneaded eraser. Then use a soft pink eraser to remove the final bits of color.

► Chalk sticks may be shaped on fine sandpaper to control their width and keep a sharp edge.

APPLYING COLORED PENCILS

Colored pencils are soft, wax-based color sticks which can be used in three basic ways. The first most common use is to produce crisp line work to delineate objects and draw in details. The second method is to tone an area; with a fairly light touch, the side of the lead of the pencil can be rubbed over the paper surface to impart a thin, transparent tone to the area. Successive layers of colors can be applied on the same area to modulate the color and value of that area. Care should be taken not to rub too hard and make shiny spots on the surface. The third technique works well for rendering details and produces bright, precise color. The designer builds up successive layers of color over an area, working in highlights and shade areas. Then he or she blends over the area with a white pencil and applies a final layer of color to increase the intensity. The result is a crisp, bright detail with a smooth uniform surface.

6
Rendering Conventions for Interior Components

All the conventions used to render objects are based upon observing light reflected off of the surfaces and finding a quick, "shorthand" method of describing the light reflection with a rendering tool such as a marker. The following are ways to describe some of the most common interior elements Additional conventions will be pointed out in the examples of professional work used in this text.

INTERIOR ELEMENTS

Floors. Floors are a ubiquitous element in an interior rendering for where walls and ceilings can be ignored, a floor must be drawn in, or everything else seems to float on the page. There are three basic strokes used to draw a floor. The first is a stroke drawn in perspective towards the vanishing point, a stroke illustrated in the floor plane of Figure 6-1. These perspective strokes establish the flat plane of the floor and visually indicate that there is a solid floor in perspective. The perspective strokes also provide the basic color for the floor. The second type is a vertical stroke used to indicate the reflections of the floor surface. Unless a floor surface is carpeted, it will show some reflections. The degree of reflectiveness is indicated by how bold and dark the vertical strokes are. For a very reflective floor, pale reflections of the objects in the interior would be rendered. However, this is rarely done as it is visually distracting and floors are seldom mirror-like. To show a reflection in a floor, one can pull a vertical stroke down from an object on the floor, the length of which should be the same as the height of the object above the reflection stroke. The value of the stroke should be light, and the color a mixture of the floor color and the color of the reflected object. The third type of stroke used to indicate a floor is a horizontal stroke, rendered at the back of the floor surface. This stroke darkens the value of the far portion of the floor so it appears to be going back in space and to be laying flat in the picture plane. This horizontal stroke can be made easily by blending markers or by using chalk.

Carpeting. The two most common conventions for indicating carpeting are created by stippling markers or by drawing a series of parallel, jagged horizontal lines. Before rendering a carpet, shade and shadow areas are outlined lightly with a pencil. When rendering, values or line weights are changed so these areas are darker than adjacent areas in full light (Fig. 6-2). Also, carpeting should become slightly darker as it recedes into the picture plane. As with hard flooring, the rendered carpet should fade out or dissolve as it reaches the forefront of the drawing. The color of the carpet is produced by rendering with a selection of the colors found in the carpet. Even if the carpet is one color, the richness of color and the variations of light and texture can be shown by using a range of colors chose in hue with the appropriate values for highlight and shadow areas. For example, a blue carpet will be rendered with light and dark blues for value (shade and shadow) changes as well as a green blue and a blue violet for richness of color. Figure 6-3 shows how these patterns and shadows are indicated by horizontal carpet lines.

The first step for the designer in the stippling technique is to put down a light-value wash of color to define where the carpet will be rendered and to establish the base color and value of the carpet. Then, with a series of very rapid dots, the carpet area is stippled with a series of colored markers starting with the lightest markers and gradually adding the darker ones. If

Figure 6–1
In this sketch the floor plane has been rendered in with marker strokes going back in perspective, and reflections in the floor have been added with vertical marker strokes.

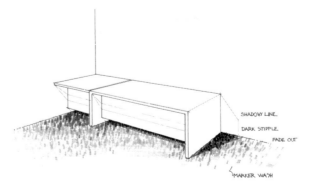

Figure 6–2
Carpet can be rendered by putting down a light wash of color and stippling darker colors to create the desired value, color, and texture.

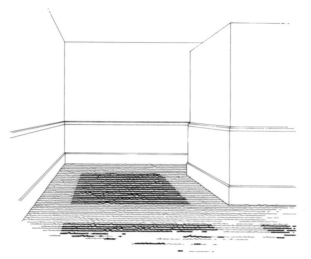

Figure 6–3
By changing the value, color, or weight of horizontal carpet lines, patterns and shadows can be indicated.

Figure 6–4
The ceilings and walls in this sketch are simply rendered with the values becoming lighter toward the edges of the image.

the carpet appears too bold or if the back portion is too bright, he or she can rub a cotton pad with chalk over the area. The chalk should be of a low intensity or a dull version of the basic carpet color.

A similar approach is used for the jagged line technique. A foundation color lighter than the carpet color is put down over the area, and then jagged horizontal lines are drawn over the area, often using a straight edge to maintain a straight path. The method used to create the jagged effect can vary from a stuttered line, made with varying pressure for a low-nap carpet, to a vertical scribble for a deep plush. The jagged lines may overlap; the lightest color is put down first and subsequently the darker ones are added. To achieve greater definition in the carpet, colored pencils can be added at the end for some crisp texture. This should be done only over a portion of the carpet area in the focal point of the rendering to suggest the texture; the viewer will understand that the texture covers the entire area. In shade areas, darker colors or heavier line weights are used which requires changing drawing tools during the length of one line or going back and drawing over a line with a darker value in the shade areas.

Ceilings and walls.

Ceilings and walls require less attention than floors; in fact, ceilings are often ignored in a rendering. Both surfaces can be indicated with a light- or neutral-value wash and line work used to indicate corners and textures. The wash should be darkest further back and become lighter as it moves forward in the picture plane. Walls are often interrupted by furniture and accessories which make it difficult to do any detailed rendering. Using a vertical stroke, the ceiling corner is rendered down to the floor, or objects rendered in front of the wall working from back to the front of the wall surface. If some texture or pattern detail is desired, it can be put in over this basic marker wash with pencil, chalk, or a darker marker although if a marker is used, it may require some line work to add definition. Ceilings are usually kept very light, and the color is applied either with horizontal strokes or in one-point perspective towards the vanishing point. As with walls, details should be faintly suggested unless they are the focal point of the drawing, a method illustrated in Figure 6-4.

Fabric.

Soft surfaces in the interior require the designer to use an intuitive, impressionistic rendering technique as a careful rendering of the folds in a fabric would be tedious and time consuming. With a few exceptions such as satin, fabrics have a mat surface, and the reflected light is diffused producing gradual value changes from highlight areas to shade areas. The folds in fabric create peaks and valleys which are rendered with highlight and shade values. When rendering fabric, the entire area is colored with the highlight value; then a middle-value color is added to the shade areas. The shade areas can be darkened progressively to achieve the desired contrast and value gradation. The transition from highlight areas to shade areas should be well blended for a soft look. The contrast in values shown in Figure 6-5 produces a satin effect. The contrast can be strong and the transition brief, but it must be blended. If the fabric has a pattern, it can be applied over the basic value with fine-point markers if the base value is light, or with pencils, chalk, or even designer's quache if strong opaque colors are needed in the pattern. A gloss or satin fabric is rendered in the same way except that the contrast is exaggerated between light and dark shades, and the value transitions are not blended.

Fabric used as upholstery is handled slightly differently from draperies and other loose fabrics because folds are fewer or nonexistent on upholstered furniture. The value changes occur between surfaces facing towards or away from the light and on a surface which is swollen or curved as part of the surface rises towards the light source and part falls away. On furniture, values are applied to the shade areas locking in the dark values, and lighter values are added to approach the highlight areas. Again, the transition between values is gradual to indicate the diffused light.

Wood. Rendering wood involves using a series of layers of color to build up color variations, grain, and highlight or shade areas. Grain lines are added as a final detailing with a fine-point marker or colored pencil. A careful observation of the grain patterns, particularly the color variations, common to different woods is helpful as these elements vary greatly in different woods. A designer should select a palette of colors ranging from a light brown to a dark brown and a dark brown or black fine-point marker with which to render the grain. When a designer selects the colors he or she must look carefully at the wood to render for the color of the very light areas and the general tone of the wood. Some woods are very warm red tones and others are cool brown tones and colors should be selected accordingly. Some accent colors are also helpful for woods like oak and maple where a yellow highlight and a deep reddish brown make good accents. For dark woods like walnut, a tan and a dark, blackish brown are good accents.

When possible, a designer should mask out the area to be rendered so the color can be applied quickly and freely. The lightest color is applied

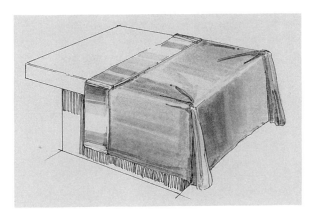

Figure 6-5
Fabric can be rendered with a gradual change of values for a soft surface or with contrast between values for a satin effect.

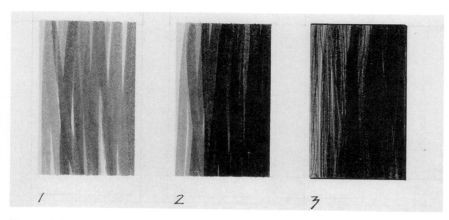

Figure 6–6
Wood is rendered by applying the color in layers and streaking it to simulate wood grain. After color is applied, dark-grain lines are added.

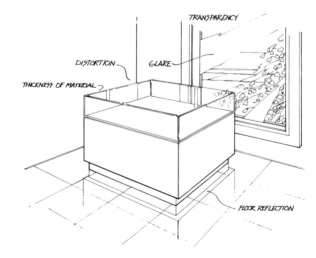

TRANSPARENCY

DISTORTION

GLARE

THICKNESS OF MATERIAL

FLOOR REFLECTION

Figure 6–7
This drawing shows the basic element involved in drawing transparent material.

over the wood area in the direction of the grain. If using markers, the strokes are overlapped to suggest the grain pattern, although some streaks of white paper should be left. Successive layers of progressively darker markers are applied using the same technique, allowing some of the lighter color to show through (Fig. 6-6). The final drawing should have gradual but contrasting changes from light to dark on the surface, and a third of the surface furthest from the viewer should be darker than the front third. Finally, the grain is reinforced with some dark line work; white line work also may be added to give the wood surface an aged appearance. When the final grain lines are drawn, the pressure is varied to produce changes in line weight along the length of the grain line.

Glass and transparency. Transparency often is considered the most difficult rendering problem, probably because a designer is asked to render what is behind the transparent object rather than the object itself. There are three basic areas of consideration when rendering transparency: first, the structure of the object as made evident in the edges and corners; second, reflections and glare on the surface of the transparent material; and third, distortions of what is seen through the transparency.

Wherever one can see the thickness of a transparent material as in the edges and corners, there will be a collection of lights, darks, and color. With clear glass, the edges show a light, cool green, but with plastic, the edges show the color of the plastic or white light. Also, the white highlights and colors in the edges of transparent materials seem to pool and flow along the edge. They are hard-edged, high-contrast areas, but they seem fluid. It is important to indicate the thickness of transparent material at the edges to give a solid structure to the material, an example of which can be seen in Figure 6-7.

Since all transparent materials are very smooth, there will be glare and strong highlights across the surface. And glare specifically can be shown with a broad streak of white that blocks the view through the material. The glare usually is found on the surface facing the light source on horizontal surfaces. Angling the glare stroke towards the viewer helps to create the illusion that the light is being reflected off of the page. Somewhat transparent reflections from interior elements also appear on the surface of glass and can be seen through to the background. Using colored pencils is the simplest way to add these reflections and should be done when the rendering is nearly complete. It is helpful to note that when the far side of a window is dark, as at night for instance, the window acts as a mirror strongly reflecting the interior. However, when the far side of the window is light, the window is transparent and reveals the outside view. Generally, colors and values are lighter and more muted in reflections and also can be rendered with less detail and precision. A suggestion of a reflection in form and color often is all that is needed.

The third element that adds to the illusion of transparency is to show the material seen through the transparency. To indicate that the viewer is looking through a material, some slight distortions near the edges along with an offset of the background lines are helpful. When looking through a curved glass, the background lines will not only be offset but will be curved, as though following the shape of the glass. Also, the intensity of color and crispness of line in the background is reduced.

Metal. The two important aspects of rendering metals are getting the color right and having the proper range of contrast on the drawing. Some metals, like chrome, are highly reflective and need strong contrasts, while others such as tarnished copper or brushed aluminum are softly reflective, requiring a narrow range of contrast. The most common metals, such as aluminum, chrome, and steel are rendered in cool gray shades with a cool, light blue accent to them. Golden or yellow metals like bronze are rendered with a rich yellow, a light golden brown brown (or ochre), and a darker warm brown. Dark metals have a particular cast to them as, for example, copper which needs a light pink for highlights and medium and dark pinkish browns for the body and reflections. Metals are usually polished to a very reflective gloss or brushed to a soft luster. These two effects are rendered very differently, and both are used in the rendering of a privacy screen in Figure 6-8.

Brushed metals. Brushed or low-luster metals require a blending of the values to show a low contrast and smooth transition from the highlight area to the darkest value. A light range of color is applied, perhaps grays number 1 through number 4 to the surface beginning with the lightest and covering the entire surface. The colors are blended as they are applied to get light streaks throughout the surface. Light values are concentrated in the highlight area to allow approximately one-third of the surface to be predominantly a dark value with only a small number of light streaks. Once the basic values are in, reflections or color tints can be added. Also, such details on the surface as fasteners can be rendered on top of this base-rendered surface.

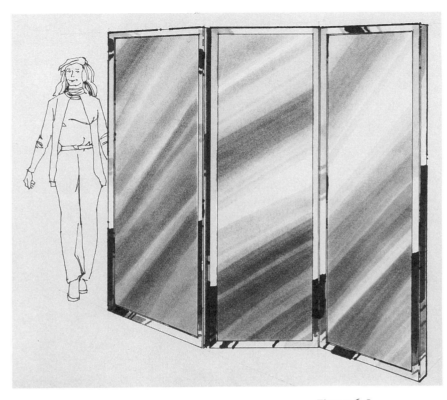

Figure 6–8
This privacy screen is rendered to indicate a brushed-metal surface with gloss metal trim. The difference when rendering the two surfaces is one of high contrast for gloss versus low contrast for the brushed surfaces.

Glossy metallic surfaces. Glossy metallic surfaces are very different from satin-finish metals in that they act like mirrors and reflect a great deal of both light and dark values. The choice of colors used in the rendering depends upon the type of metal. In light metals such as steel, reflections are done in a lighter value of the object being reflected whereas in dark metals such as copper, light and dark reflections are done in the metal colors without picking up specific reflected color. The following are some guidelines for developing a glossy surface:

▶ Decide on a major, dark reflection area and a smaller "sympathetic" or similar dark reflection.

▶ Very lightly, pencil an outline around the highlight areas and any spot highlights; if possible, these areas will be left unrendered. They may be put in later with white opaque paint or chalk, if necessary.

▶ Keep high contrasts between light and dark areas. The light areas will carry the "color" of the metal so they will predominate. Avoid many middle values.

▶ Round or "flow" the edges of the dark areas so that they pool on the surface or run along the edges.

▶ Thin and draw out dark colors along long, thin surfaces and edges. Let them thicken at corners.

▶ Keep dark values off of the outside edge of an object as light halos belong there.

▶ Reflected color may be added with chalk or colored pencil in the same manner the basic values were added.

Plants and foliage. House plants, trees, shrubs, and other foliage each have their own overall shape, a unique growth pattern for leaves and branches, and a definite leaf size and shape. To indicate a plant in an interior, lightly sketch the overall shape of the plant to serve as a reminder and guide when applying the color. Select stem colors, tan and warm brown for example, and draw the trunk or main stems of the plant. Two ways of sketching foliage are indicated in Figure 6-9. When sketching, keep in mind the general pattern or growth direction of the branches and, with a broken line, draw the major branches. Note that some plants grow with arching, gothic-type branches and some with crooked, tortured branches. The broken-branch lines leave open areas along the branches for foliage to be added pictorially in front of the branch. Keep the branches within the general shape of the plant which was sketched lightly earlier. Select three values of the foliage color, probably in a warm green range. Using a short stroke which, if possible, simulates the size and shape of the leaf, add foliage around the stem and branches loosely keeping to the shape of the plant. Use the darkest value primarily in the shade side of the plant and on the underside of the branches. Use the light value in the upper and highlight areas, and fill with the middle value; this will result in a rendering of the basic plant. Now with chalk, which is opaque and will cover background elements, add some highlight foliage that is not attached to the plant to effervesce above the highlight area. The branches and trunk also may need some fine line work on the shade side for definition.

Volumes in an interior.

The simplest way to render a form is to define a light source, and show how different parts and sides of that form are affected by the light. In two-point perspective there are three primary-value surfaces and a shadow area. Regardless of the color of the object or the surface pattern, the designer will have to establish a value range for the object. This rendering can be done in gray shades or in the value range selected by the palette of colors for a specific color. The following three primary factors determine the value range for rendering an object:

1. The intensity and directness of the light. Strong, direct light such as sunlight, will wash out surfaces facing the light and create a dark shade side and a harsh shadow. For this lighting situation, a wide range of values will be needed with the highlights extremely pale and the contrasts high. As the intensity of the light decreases, the values will become darker, and there will be less contrast. The highlight area is rendered closer in color to the pigment color of the object, and a narrower and slightly darker range of values is needed.

2. The color of the object. Of course, dark objects require a dark range of values, and light objects require a light range. To choose the range, select the pigment or object color of the item to be rendered and add the lighter and darker values close to it. The number of values selected or the length of the value range used will depend upon the light condition, but a large range is used for strong direct light.

Figure 6–9
These sketches show two ways to indicate plant foliage. Use chalk when drawing foliage over another rendered surface.

Figure 6–10
The front box in this drawing is rendered to have a dull, reflective surface by using strong contrasts and stroking the markers vertically on the top surface. The second box is rendered a light value with low contrast to indicate a non-reflective surface.

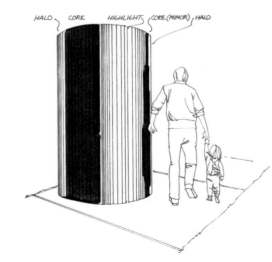

HALO CORE HIGHLIGHT CORE (MINOR) HALO

Figure 6–11a
This diagram shows the location of highlight and dark areas on a cylinder.

3. The reflectiveness of an object (Fig. 6-10). This affects the contrast of the object and, as such, the number of values needed to render the object. A highly reflective surface will pick up and reflect both light and dark areas from the environment. Dark, reflective objects therefore, will be rendered primarily with dark values with some very light reflections in them and with high contrast. And a dark, dull surface will not have the very light values reflected in its surfaces.

The problem, then, is to determine which surfaces are light and which are dark, which range of values to use, and how strong will be the contrast. Normally, the top surface or surfaces of an object are the lightest value. The front surface, which is not in full light facing into the room, is the mid-value surface. The side or back surface is the darkest value; it is also adjacent to the shadow area. Since the shadow area is only the lack of direct light on the floor or ground surface, it is not totally dark. Therefore, it is not black and may often be lighter than the shade side of a dark object. However, once the basic value system has been assigned to an object, some variation of value occurs on each surface. This surface variation is a shorthand way of indicating the complexities of reflected light from the room which falls on the object. Each surface has a gradation in value from one edge to another, and light edges on one surface are adjacent to dark edges on another surface. On cylinders, the darkest values are near the vertical edges, called the *core color* on the curved surface. The core areas do not reach the edge, however; this is where some reflected light strikes the cylinder. It is called a *halo* as it glows slightly between the edge and the dark core area.

To speed the application of markers or other color medium, a light outline of the shadow areas and highlights can be drawn with a common graphite pencil. The application of color can be very careful and precise, covering the entire surface, or it may loosely suggest values and color with much of the surface unrendered. The diagram of a cylinder in Figures 6-11a and 6-11b show how values are used to show highlighted and dark areas.

Shadows. Shadows are important elements in rendering interiors for the variation they give to surfaces, including the enhanced feeling of light or atmosphere, the added depth of space, and the setting off, through contrast, of the highlight areas. Shadows may be plotted with perspective-construction systems or suggested with an intuitive general placement. Because shadows are a result of blocked light on a surface, they are rendered with a dark shade value of the color of the surface the shadow falls across. The color is applied with the same stroke and texture as that portion of the surface not in the shadow. Shadows also fade as they move away from an object due to secondary-light sources or reflected light. Figure 6-12 shows how the shadows cast can take on surface textures. For relatively light shadows, a gray marker can be applied over a rendered area, but one must be cautious as too much gray over other colors can muddy and dull a rendering. Shadows for plants and small objects are usually very light and suggested with a few rapid, gestured strokes. But shadows for large objects or major elements in an interior should be plotted or carefully sketched in as such important shadows can make a drawing look odd if not put in correctly. Small shadows also fall from arms on a couch, table legs, and such. These shadows help greatly in reading the surface of the objects and setting the different spatial planes apart.

Patterns. Surface patterns are usually drawn in over a base color for an object. There are two ways to select the base color; the example of rendering a carpet will make these different methods clear. If there is either a light background color to the carpet or a dominant background color, that color will be the base color for the rendering. On a carpet with no discernible background color, there will be an overall visual color effect, for example, a rose color made up of red, tan, yellow, orange, and some blue yarns woven together. This overall effect will serve as the base color. The base color of the carpet is rendered in to set the texture, light, shade, and shadow areas. The base color is kept a bit lighter than the final value effect desired in the rendered carpet. Now the pattern is added: If a red stripe is desired, the red will be pink in the highlight areas and will range to a deep red or burgundy in the shadow areas. Figure 6-13 demonstrates the use of progressive color to render a pattern. Keep in mind the texture and value areas as the pattern colors are rendered in.

Corners, edges, and thresholds. Often overlooked in an interior rendering but something that can add a great deal of perceived detail with very little rendering work is the handling of edges, corners, or thresholds. In this instance, thresholds refer to the separation or transition line between two separate surfaces or materials. Often these boundary lines are indicated by a single black line which does not offer much information about the texture, size, or material that cause the boundary line. When two surfaces meet, there are two edges to deal with: One edge which recedes from the light

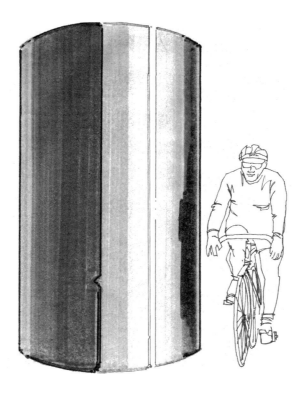

Figure 6–11b
This sketch of a cylinder shows how the values are blended from the highlight areas to the dark-core areas. The values lighten again in the halo areas on the edges of the cylinder.

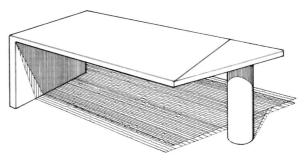

Figure 6–12
Two shadows are cast by this table from separate light sources. The shadow takes on the texture of the surface it falls across.

should be drawn dark; the other edge which faces the light will create a light highlight line (Fig. 6-14). The distance between the edges can be shown also. A tight fit will be composed of two thin, close lines, one dark, one light. When there is a gap, the threshold will be bold and can be drawn as a dark gray line. These boundary lines are also places where accent colors collect. For instance, a room's corner facing the light might be a highlight edge with a yellow cast to it and a shade edge on a table leg may pick up some lavender as a reflection from another room element. The edges in an interior also may cast narrow shadows. A fine-point gray marker will indicate these very effectively. By dealing with the corners, edges, and thresholds as important details, the viewer gets a sense of the construction and a feeling that real materials are planned for the interior rather than a feeling that the rendering is a perspective-block diagram of the interior.

Figure 6–13
Patterns are rendered by putting down a light-base color and adding darker colors in the patterns of the design. This sketch has been left unfinished to show the wash of color and progressive layers of pattern colors.

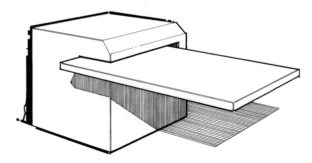

Figure 6–14
Each edge of the table in this sketch has been drawn to suggest highlights, shadows, or the spaces between other surfaces.

7
Full-Color Rendering

In order to produce a full-color rendering the designer must change focus from the design of the interior to the idea of producing a visual aid to present the design ideas. The rendering process is no longer a component of the visual dialogue which helps the designer to resolve design concerns for the interior. Rather, the designer has made the decision to present the completed interior. The thinking that goes into the rendering will be concerned with its drawing technique rather than with the design content. The process of producing a full-color rendering can be broken down into three phases. (See color plates 1-6.)

PHASE I: PREPARATION

Before any rendering can be done, some basic decisions must be made. The first is paper choice, and three characteristics of paper are important when selecting one for a marker rendering. The first is surface because a paper should take a marker well and show a clean, bright color. The second is absorbency as the marker should dry quickly and with little bleeding. The third is color; the paper color should complement the marker colors and the interior.

Four types of paper work well, although each has its own advantages and disadvantages.

Vellum is a translucent paper which does not bleed at all and has the unique advantage of being able to be worked from the back side. That is, marker strokes or chalk on the back side of the paper will show through although with a subdued tone. For example, a black marker used on the back side of vellum will show through as a number 7 gray, effective for putting in shadows and for darkening an area. Vellum also has a soft surface which accepts chalk and colored pencils well. The drawbacks to vellum are a slow drying time for markers; colors are not as strong as they are on more absorbent papers; and multiple layers of marker washes turn muddy and leave blotches.

Marker-layout paper is a thin, white, fairly opaque paper made to accept marker dye with little bleeding. The colors will be strong but light. Unfortunately, this paper does not accept chalk well, even when the surface is prepared with talc. The paper is thin enough to trace through although a light box is sometimes needed. Colored-marker paper is a heavy paper that takes markers, chalk, and pencil very well but its absorbency causes some bleeding of the marker, so all fine work must be done with pencil, ink, and chalk. The color of the paper can be chosen to complement the color scheme of the interior. On this paper, highlights and bright areas can be added with chalk, pencil, and white, opaque paint.

Diazo and photocopy papers are very absorbent papers used in reproduction processes. Clearly their advantage is having the basic interior-line drawing reproduced without tracing or transferring it from another sheet. Multiple copies of the interior-line drawing can be made, and each can be rendered differently showing design changes or various color options, and with photocopies, the size of the line drawing can also be adjusted. Diazo prints can be made with a background; the most common is a sepia or brownline print with a background tone of brown which can be rendered as a colored paper. The primary drawback to print papers is the absorbency which causes excessive bleeding of the marker dye and requires careful application and a reworking of the line drawing.

The next decision when preparing for a rendering is the color palette to be used. For each color in the interior, a series of values in that color are needed. For instance, to put in a blue chair one will need a light blue, a medium blue, and a dark blue, but in addition, accent colors will be needed, such as pale yellow for incandescent lights, pale blue for chrome, and perhaps a lilac for reflected accents. Finally, it is important to test the markers on a strip of the same paper on which the drawing will be rendered. This test strip will show the chromatic strength of the markers on that paper, as well as how much bleeding will occur, and how deep of a color a double layer of a particular marker will make. This strip then will serve as a reference during the rendering for marker selection. To make the test strip, series of boxes are drawn and filled, each with a different marker color; then half of the area is gone over in each box with a second coat of the color.

PHASE II: SETTING UP THE RENDERING

The designer's goal when setting up a rendering is to finish with a clean, light-line drawing on the desired paper ready for the application of color and enhanced line weights. The consideration that goes into planning the drawing and the rendering of that line drawing must include the composition and size of the drawing and, subsequently, the choice of perspective view. To aid in this decision, one should try to jot down the purpose of the drawing to help set priorities for the drawing and to understand how it fits into the total presentation. Then a designer should make a series of thumbnail sketches to visualize the composition and to guide the choice of perspective system that will be used to construct the line drawing.

Once a perspective layout for the interior has been drawn, a light source or light sources must be chosen and shadow and shade areas added to the drawing. This should be done lightly with a pencil to serve as a reminder when markers are applied. And in a similar manner, locations for reflections, edge details, textures, and patterns should be penciled in. The development of the perspective-line drawing will be a series of overlays: On each successive overlay, more detail will be added and unnecessary construction lines eliminated. When the final perspective is ready, it needs to be transferred to the chosen rendering paper by tracing, transfer, or photomechanical means, a method demonstrated in Color plate 2. The transferred drawing will likely need some correction and tightening with ellipse guides and other drawing aids. On this drawing, light pencil lines should be included for such effects of light as shadows and reflections. At this point various line weights can be added although line weights can be added at the finish of the drawing as well. It is a good idea to add dark lines sparingly at first, for a good rendering relies less on line work and more on surface rendition. With a line drawing in place and a color test strip prepared, color can be applied to the paper.

PHASE III: APPLICATION OF COLOR

From the color test strip a designer will get a good idea of the value range of the markers he or she will be using. Because light markers can always be made darker while the reverse is not true, it is best to work from light to dark when putting down marker colors (Color plate 3). Start with the largest areas and lay down a light wash of color to cover the entire area except for any strong highlights, until the area is filled, or until the color fades out to the edges of the paper. Go back into that area with the darker values, and add texture and surface modulation, and leave light areas for reflections. Continue this process of working from large areas to small areas until all the basic marker application is done and each surface and value is described. Most of the highlights should now be in the drawing along with the textures, material indications, and surface patterns. But, as Color plate 4 shows, some work is still needed. At this point the rendering may look out of focus because the markers do not produce crisp edges or tend to bleed slightly and blend together. This is very natural and is expected because markers are both "gross" tools and "generalists" when it comes to describing details. To crisp up a drawing, add or darken the shadows and shade areas to boost the contrast in the drawing and make the highlights and the focal point visually stronger.

The greatest aid for clearer definition will be the addition of fine line work. Color plate 5 reflects the improvements that may be made. Add lines where needed to define edges, enhance textures and patterns, and reinforce the perspective. Sometimes a fine, dark line along a highlight will crisp the highlight and add the necessary contrast to "pop" the highlight and make it seem bright. Colored pencils and chalks now can be added to modulate colors and tone surfaces. Finally, white opaque can be added for spot highlights (Color plate 6).

When rendering on colored paper, the procedure is slightly different primarily because the paper acts as a middle value in the rendering and not the highlight value as when rendering on white paper. The following steps are recommended for colored-paper rendering.

STEP-BY-STEP COLORED-PAPER RENDERING

1. Select a paper color, preferably a predominant color within the interior, and a slightly lighter shade than the middle value of that color. This allows one to work with lighter and darker shades when rendering.

2. Transfer the line drawing to the colored paper and tighten up the transferred-line drawing with drawing guides. Any lines that will be covered with dark markers can be drawn with a metallic colored pencil which will show through the dark marker.

3. Put in the "value keys" to determine where the lightest and darkest areas will be, and leave the rest of the drawing the paper color. Remember one can always lighten the light areas with chalk and pencil, and darken the dark areas with marker. One should play it safe at this point and refrain from too great a contrast.

4. Adjust the middle values with marker or chalk to indicate plane changes, shade areas, distance from the viewer, and effects of light.

5. Do some minimal line work with a fine-point pen and colored pencils to define shapes and details.

6. Render in patterns and textures, and add subtle reflections.

7. Increase contrasts where needed to emphasize important elements.

8. Add detail to surfaces with line work and increase color intensity with colored pencils, opaque paint, and chalk.

9. Put in final highlights with white opaque; do not overdo it and remember that not all highlights are the same intensity or size. A silver pencil makes a good highlight edge in dark areas as it resists absorbing the marker dye and reflects light.

The designer will notice from his or her marker-test strip that marker color fades slightly as it is absorbed into the colored paper. It is dark when applied but lightens noticeably after a few minutes.

The final element to a full-color rendering is the presentation of the drawing on the page. A border of a few inches of paper should be left around the drawing, and a title block including a bottom-margin line will help identify the drawing and visually tie it into the other drawing included in the presentation. Because of the time involved in producing a full-color rendering, minor changes or design options can be made by rendering the changes on a separate sheet, cutting them out, and either pasting them in position on the rendering, or pasting on a clear-acetate overlay on top of the rendering.

8

Techniques for Effective Presentations

Renderings and presentation sketches themselves cannot effectively convey the design of an interior space. A complete presentation package has to include a variety of visualization tools with each method used describing a different aspect of the interior. In addition to the presentation package, there is the transmission package of detailed drawings for the construction, purchase, installation, and specification of all the elements in the interior. The concern here is putting together a presentation effective both in content and in visual organization.

CONTENT: TYPES OF VISUALIZATION TOOLS

Floor Plan

This is usually the central element of any presentation and one to which all other elements refer. The floor plan should be large enough to clearly show details and furniture. If possible, it should include not only the building structure but also the immediate environment around the building to provide information about exterior views, major traffic-flow sources, and adjoining structures.

This does not have to be a site plan, but enough of the environment should be shown to indicate related adjacent spaces. Floor plans can be used, perhaps at a reduced scale, to diagram traffic flow, lighting plans, significant space organizations, carpet and flooring schemes, and the like.

Specialized Plan Drawings

Reflected ceiling plans and other plan drawings will be used in a presentation only if they show some significant design feature that cannot be indicated in a perspective or elevation drawing.

Elevations and Section Views

Wall elevations and sections are useful to show site lines, layout and graphic patterns, and changes in surface heights. They should be specific in their purpose and not be a substitute for a perspective or axonometric drawing.

Axonometric Drawings

These are very good for describing the volumes in a space and should be used when the volumes or the placement of volumes is important, such as in a colonnade.

Perspective Drawings

Perspective drawings are the most visually appealing type of drawings. A color rendering often is useful to display and show interested parties how the new interior will look. In addition to being a showpiece, perspective drawing can consist of small vignettes used to illustrate specific design elements or details in the interior. Using perspective vignettes also helps a designer to build confidence for rendering.

Scale Models or Mockups

A scale model is probably the most efficient way to communicate space, volume, and the positioning of masses in the interior. Fully detailed models which show color and pattern are very time-consuming and are seldom done.

Drawings of the Exterior Architecture

Interiors are often closely related to their exterior architecture or the entrance façade. Because of this relationship, it is helpful to show a color elevation of the exterior as a reference for the interior design.

Sample Boards

Sample boards are very useful for giving an impression of the color, texture, and overall feel for the surfaces in the interior. They require a sensitive and ordered graphic layout, where the color and samples have such strong visual presence that without careful layout, these boards can very easily become distracting.

Special Features

Unique architectural features, custom furniture, or other special features of an interior should be highlighted in a presentation. This can be done with a perspective vignette or an enhanced orthographic elevation. This drawing will be subordinate to the major rendering and can be coordinated nicely with the sample board or other special feature drawings.

Graphic Details

An aspect of an interior that is sometimes overlooked is the choice of a graphic system for signage, identification, and information. Too often this is left without thoughtful consideration, yet some form of graphics will appear throughout most interiors. Designing or specifying an appropriate signage system can mean the difference between a delightful detail or an annoying blemish on a surface. A graphics board can be a very simple presentation of the typography and physical system for the signage.

Given that there are so many elements to an interior and, additionally, there are a host of ways to describe and explain the design of the interior, the organization of the presentation is critical to its success. The first step in providing order to a presentation is to prepare a script. A simple story board, similar to those used to present ideas for television commercials, is very effective for organizing a presentation (Fig. 8-1). The general plan for a presentation is to show the overall design concept featuring the major space, often done with a perspective rendering and floor plan. From these, the organizational concept and the function of the interior are described, addressing the design priorities which were established with the client at the onset of the project. Then special features, materials, and other spaces should be described. Detailed information such as a materials schedule, cost accounting, and implementation program can be prepared as a handout for the client.

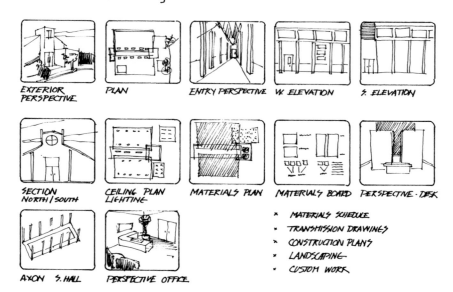

SAUBER FOUNDATION PROJECT

EXTERIOR PERSPECTIVE   PLAN   ENTRY PERSPECTIVE   W. ELEVATION   S. ELEVATION

SECTION NORTH/SOUTH   CEILING PLAN LIGHTING   MATERIALS PLAN   MATERIALS BOARD   PERSPECTIVE · DESK

AXON S. HALL   PERSPECTIVE OFFICE

- × MATERIALS SCHEDULE
- × TRANSMISSION DRAWINGS
- × CONSTRUCTION PLANS
- × LANDSCAPING
- × CUSTOM WORK

Figure 8-1
A story board such as this one helps to plan and organize a presentation to clearly communicate design ideas.

VISUAL ORGANIZATION
OF A PRESENTATION

The hallmarks of a good visual presentation are clarity of purpose, consistent graphic style, an overall organizational structure, and unifying presentation mounts or backgrounds. A professional presentation shows that the designer has respect for his work and for the client. This attitude carries over, and the work is seen to be worthy of careful consideration. Regardless of the level of the sophistication of the drawings, if they are handled well and the presentation is carefully designed, the content of the presentation will be considered with the same care and professionalism.

A presentation can be made to appear very formal or very casual. But regardless of this presentation attitude, the same principles for organization apply: It is in the execution that an attitude is developed.

Clarity of Purpose

Clarity of purpose relates directly to the previous discussion of the importance of an organizational script for the presentation. With a script describing the presentation sequence of the information and with set priorities, the designer knows which information is important and new and which information is supportive. He or she then can set about making this visually clear to the viewer. Drawings have distinct visual-information content, and they can be enhanced to emphasize more emphatically certain information. There is a general hierarchy to the sequence of presentation, moving from general and impressionistic ideas to the specific details. For example, a presentation may start out with a perspective of the space, both to show the character of the space and to capture the viewer's attention. Then a floor plan is presented to show the organization of the space and its performance capabilities. This may include enhanced floor plans to show furniture or traffic flow or, perhaps, security controls. Following the plan of the space, details of small areas such as elevations or material selection can be shown. Finally, schedules for furniture, construction, and such are presented to answer specific questions.

Some designs are fairly complex and when this is the case, the highest design priorities can be highlighted so they become visually apparent, and related design elements should be grouped and presented together. For ex-

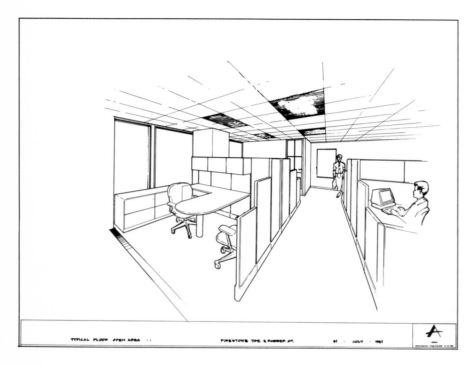

Figure 8–2
This sketch shows how a minimal title block can be applied to drawings as a consistent unifying device when presenting work. *PHH Avenue, Chicago, IL.*

ample, discussions about space, traffic flow, site lines, and room capacity all may be related and presented together.

It is worth noting that the designer is often immersed in the project and can make the mistake of assuming that the viewer knows as much about the design as he or she does, or that the viewer can read all of the designer's ideas from a few drawings. The content of any particular drawing is limited and, rather than trying to discuss all aspects of an interior with a few drawings, the designer should take advantage of the directed nature of drawings, focusing them for the particular design purpose. This will mean producing more drawings for the presentation, and increasing the overall effectiveness of the presentation.

Consistent Graphic Style

The graphic style of a series of drawings includes such elements as the drawing style, use of color and materials, typography, and the boldness of the line work. Consistency does not mean that all elements should be the same, but they should be handled in a similar manner from drawing to drawing. If a colored floor plan is included with a perspective-marker rendering, it makes sense to use a marker or other source for clear, bright colors on the floor plan. The line work used on plan drawings, elevations, and perspective vignettes should be similar and consistent in range of boldness and line quality.

Even drawings that are seen to have set standards for execution allow for variation. The dimensions of a plan drawing or the line weight or the lettering used are all variables that should be consistent from drawing to drawing. Typically, the style used on the major drawings, such as the plan drawings, sets the style of the other drawings.

Organizational Structure

Organizational structure is the format of the individual drawings and their relationship to each other. Each drawing has to be positioned on the page, margins have to be established, and a title block must be added. Figure 8-2 shows how a title block can unify the finished drawing. If a grid or standard format is established, not only is there a greater coherence from drawing to drawing, but the setting-up time of the drawing is also faster as format decisions have already been made and become routine. An organizational structure should address all issues of presentation from margin size to the question of permitting or not the use of overlap for positioning drawings and materials (Fig. 8-3). A simple system for a presentation can be established by first selecting acceptable paper sizes. For example, 9-by-12, 14-by-18, 18-by-24, or 24-by-36-inches. As with these paper dimensions, the sizes selected should be related in some way and should be functional dimensions, either proportional to each other, multiples of each other, common paper sizes, or even standard photocopy sizes.

Next a grid should be drawn on each permissible sheet size. The grid can be very simple, showing margins and title block location, or very elaborate with many subdivisions for the placement and alignment of type, small drawings, materials, and other elements. A gimmick also can be incorporated into the format, such as a gestured line stroke across the bottom of each page. Or, as in Figure 8-4, torn paper could be used on the title block. The format will ensure it is used throughout the presentation in a consistent manner. Also, these format grids will serve as underlays for the positioning of drawings and other presentation materials.

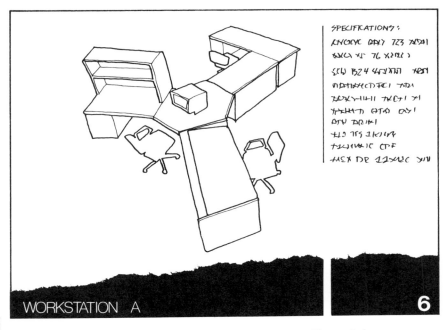

Figure 8–4
Often a simple gimmick like this torn paper title block will add to the graphic quality of a presentation.

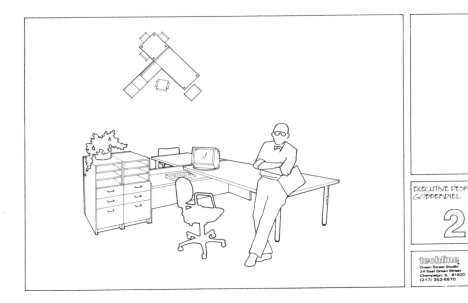

Figure 8–3
The organizational structure used in this drawing ensures a consistent format for presentation. There is a standard margin, type style, and title block. There is also an invisible grid which controls the placement of the small-plan drawing and the perspective. *Paul Loduha, Techline, Inc., Champaign, IL.*

Unifying Mounts and Backgrounds

Some presentations are for groups large enough to require that the drawings be mounted to be easily presented. Mounted drawings offer some distinct advantages when one is presenting design ideas. The mount board informally frames the drawing and thus separates it from the immediate environment and neutralizes distracting backgrounds. The designer controls the frame size, color, and shape, which is an opportunity to unify further a series of drawings into one coherent presentation. There are many offices which have set formats for mounting drawings, typically with a series of standard board sizes all in the same color. A drawing is mounted on a board to leave at least a 2-inch margin, and the company symbol or a business card is adhered to the lower-right-hand corner of the board. Presentation mounts can become rather elaborate, even decorative, but one should avoid making them look as though more effort went into the mount than into the drawings. The best rule is to keep mounts simple and neutral in color and applied graphics. Mounting a drawing and cutting a window mat to go over it is usually reserved for drawings which will go on public display or are highly developed renderings which deserve formal, careful treatment.

There are a few common methods for mounting drawings, each with certain advantages and drawbacks, and some drawings need a little preparation before mounting. For example, the color of the mount board will show through a rendering on translucent vellum or trace. To prevent this, spray the back of the vellum with flat-white lacquer paint; this also will brighten the highlights in the drawing. Drawings should be trimmed square before mounting. Also, diazo prints should be run through the developer cycle twice to prevent fading of the drawing. The following are the most common methods for mounting drawings.

Drymount. Drymount tissue is a sheet of dry adhesive that is sandwiched between the drawing and the mount board. It is put in a heat press, and the drawing is permanently mounted. This process requires special equipment, and the drawings cannot be unmounted. A similar product is available that does not use heat, and hence requires no special equipment. It is a sheet of double-stick tissue that is applied to the back of the drawing, and the drawing is adhered to the mount board. This system requires very careful handling and is recommended only for heavy papers as thin papers will wrinkle easily. When correctly done, both mounting tissues present drawings with a very smooth and flat surface. They offer the cleanest overall appearance.

Spray adhesive. The back of a drawing can be sprayed and mounted to a board with adhesive. A strong adhesive should be used as sprays with low adhesion, such as positionable spray adhesives, will allow the drawing to move with humidity change and wrinkle. Sprays are somewhat messy due to overspray, and the mount is permanent. They are more convenient than mounting tissue; however, the surface of the mount may not be flat and smooth.

Border tape. A one-quarter-inch mat-black tape can be used to mount a drawing by taping it down around the edges of the paper. Putting the tape down carefully so it is straight will produce a black border line between the drawing and the mount board, a very acceptable graphic device. Drawings mounted in this way can be unmounted by trimming the edges, but since the entire drawing is not fixed to the board some surface variation will be apparent in the sheet. This is not usually distracting. However, if tape is used only at the corners, the uneven paper surface is more apparent and can be annoying.

Double-stick tape. A strip of double-stick tape can be used in much the same way as border tape, but it is unnoticeable and works very well with heavy papers. With thin papers, however, it is unsatisfactory as it is very apparent where the tape has been used and does not offer the opportunity of using the tape as a graphic device.

The color of mat board used for mounting drawings should be a neutral; shades of gray, brown, and tan work the best. Stronger or more striking colors, including black and white, tend to require a great deal of coordination with the drawings and often will still overpower the color subtlety of the drawings.

To coordinate the drawings being mounted, the boards can be sized to complement each other. This may be as straightforward as keeping all mount-board heights at 24 inches. Drawings will be placed on the board with a two-inch top and side margin, leaving the bottom margin to fluctuate. The width of each board will be four inches wider than the drawing being mounted. Another system is to have all boards cut in a proportion similar to each other (Fig. 8-5).

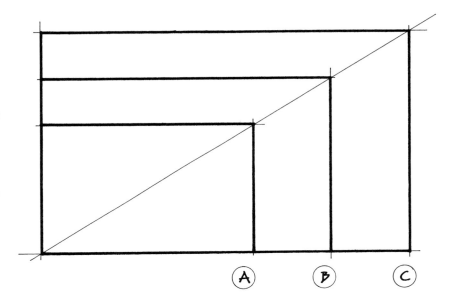

Figure 8–5
Rectangles A, B, and C are all the same proportion since they all have a common diagonal. This is one way to coordinate different paper sizes so they appear to belong together.

For example, if the standard or most commonly used size is 18-by-24 inches, boards of different sizes but in the same proportion can be derived by drawing a diagonal through opposing corners of the 18-by-24-inch board. Now any board size with a similar diagonal will be proportional to 18-by-24 inches.

There are some graphic devices which can be used on mount boards. The most common is the company logotype. An identification system may be used such as the numbering of the board or the color coding of the board with a strip of colored tape. Sometimes the graphic device is also very decorative, as for example, a torn-paper edge applied to the bottom of each board. This torn edge may be repeated in blueprints and other support drawings by printing them with a torn piece of paper attached.

Presentation mounts can also help coordinate models and drawings. The mat board used for the drawings could be used as a base for the model, perhaps in the construction of the model. This may seem like a minor consideration, but it is effective.

The illustration of design concepts through drawings and scale models is probably the most efficient and cost-effective presentation technique available to designers. Careful selection of drawings along with a thoughtful sequence of presentation and presentation format are key elements to successful communication with a client. This form of presentation is also comfortable for the designer, as drawings and sketch models are natural products of the design process.

The development of drawing skills needed for presentations can and should take advantage of the fact that they are a part of the process of designing. Early in this text, the relationship between drawing and thinking was discussed. It was pointed out then that as design ideas become more concrete, the drawings become progressively more detailed. In the early stages of designing, loose sketching is desired and a variety of perhaps unrelated details are explored, and at this stage, a variety of drawing techniques also may be employed. It is during this early, ambiguous design phase that the designer can attempt new drawing techniques and can pick up skills that will be useful for presentation sketching.

Later stages of design, however, require more accurate and detailed drawings. They should be of a consistent style, and the important design aspects of the new interior must be described with drawings. Having experimented with techniques and styles earlier in the project, the designer can select those that are comfortable and appropriate for desired communication. These techniques can be employed in the later phases of design and serve as preliminary drawings for the final presentation drawings. This is a natural way to develop drawing skills, where the designer works from loose sketching with progressive refinement to the presentation drawings. It allows the design process and the drawing process to work together, reenforcing each other. For example, a finished-presentation drawing cannot be forced; the design thinking has to be there, or the drawing will lack convincing detail and form information. However, by attempting a more finished drawing, the designer is forced to ask design questions and, perhaps more importantly, to answer them.

Another approach which facilitates learning to produce presentation sketches of interiors is to reduce the complexities of drawing an interior into manageable parts. The rendering of individual interior components can be seen as a vocabulary of basic-rendering conventions which may be used to "build" the interior. Using this method, the designer can add progressively to his or her skills and progress from enhanced orthographic drawings to line perspectives and value drawings to elaborate color renderings if that is what is called for.

A final component to making presentation drawings is having a mental model of what presentation drawings should look like, something that is more important than most people realize. Without a mental model of what one is trying to achieve in a drawing, the results are most often overly self-conscious and awkward. In the attempt to make the drawing perfect without knowing what perfect is, one is doomed to failure. This failure also discourages the designer from attempting more drawings and he or she begins to feel that he or she just cannot do it. The portfolio section of this text contains drawings from professional architectural and design offices. The drawings range from very casual thumbnail sketches to elaborate color renderings. They illustrate the full range of the type of drawings a designer might do, with an emphasis on showing a range of presentation drawings from simple to complex, and offer models for making presentation drawings. They also show that drawings used to present design ideas need not be an artist's or illustrator's rendition of an interior but that clear sketches or renderings by a designer can serve very well as presentation drawings.

It is worth restating that rendering interiors is a special skill, just as portrait drawing is a special skill. When considered as such, and the conventions used in rendering interiors are understood, the task of learning to produce effective interior-presentation drawings is made much simpler. Anyone involved in the design process of creating interior spaces can learn to produce interior renderings.

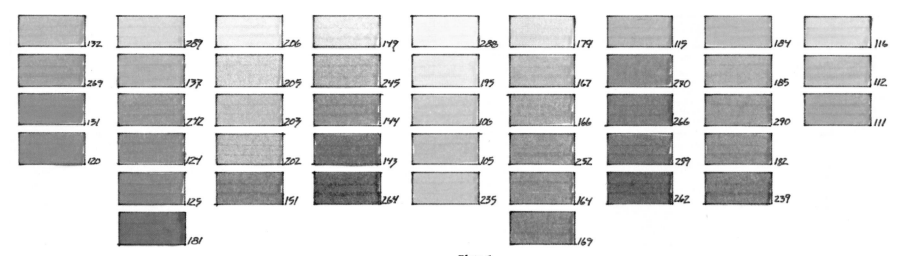

Plate 1
Color-maker test sheet showing the selection of markers for various hues, each arranged from light to dark values. This represents an essential palette of colors for rendering colors.

Plate 2
A perspective construction of the interior to be rendered has been enlarged on a copy machine to the desired size. This is a tracing of the perspective enlargement, and it will serve as an underlay for the rendering.

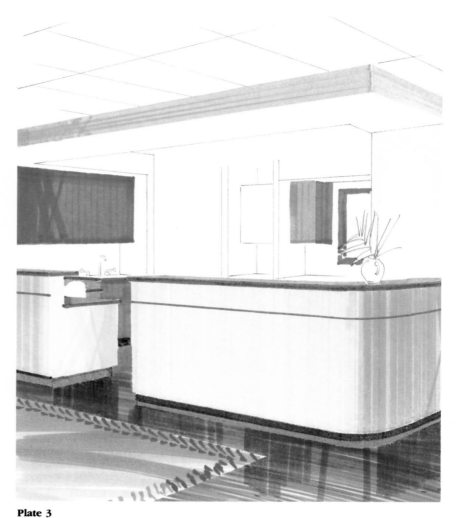

Plate 3
A light-pencil-line drawing was made from drawing plate 20. The first step in rendering the interior is to apply markers to the major surfaces in the interior, keeping in mind light and dark values.

Plate 4
All the basic marker work has been done in this drawing and line work is needed to make the marker strokes appear crisper and to define edges.

Plate 5
Line work has been added using a variety of line weights and a combination of graphite pencil and ink. Also some shadows have been added with gray markers.

Plate 6
The contrast has been enhanced in this final stage by going over some areas with darker values. Chalk and colored pencil have also been applied to tone areas and add some small details of strong color.

Plate 7

In the sketch above the perspective-line work going to the right-vanishing point can be seen through the rendering. Because of the lightness of the construction lines and the heavy use of lines throughout the drawing, they are not distracting. Textures on the flooring are suggested in areas, and they fade to the edges of the rendering. Floor reflections are shown with light-blue vertical strokes, suggesting wall reflections.

Armstrong World Industries, Lancaster, PA. Project: Nursery by Louise Kostich Cowan.
Medium: Felt markers.

Plate 8

In the detail, above right, the clothing on the closet door is done with line work and a stroke of color added; a shadow is also included on the far side of the dress. Items in the closet are suggested with a quick stroke of color and line work.

Armstrong World Industries, Lancaster, PA. Project: (detail of 9-2a) Medium: Felt markers.

Plate 9

Notice the streak of light across the oak wardrobe, rendered by changing values from a deep brown to a very light tan. A pattern is suggested on the quilt with dabs of red, red-violet, burnt umber, and some quick line work. Shadows are placed under the bed, and the shade side of objects are dark and in contrast to front surfaces. Line work is strong and delineates most objects in the room. Details are merely suggested. The viewer is led into this drawing by looking over the railing.

Armstrong World Industries, Lancaster, Pa. Project: American oak interior by Louisa Kostich Cowan. Medium: Felt markers.

Plate 10

This drawing shows strong, dominant flooring. Reflections are suggested by the light streaks on either side of the island counter. Yellow marker is put around lights for a soft glow, and plants are suggested with loose, disconnected, marker jabs. This drawing has a strong feeling of light due to the contrasts both in value and the dominant blue and orange contrast of the composition.

Armstrong World Industries, Lancaster, Pa. Project: Kitchen and living room by Louisa Kostich Cowan. Medium: Felt markers.

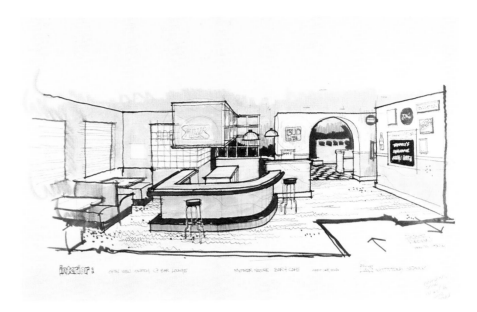

Plate 11

The drawing on the right is a view of the same interior shown in color plate 12. The viewer is looking through the front wall of the building to the bar area. Notice how the outside edges of the drawing disolve into the white of the paper.

Albitz Design, Inc., Minneapolis, MN. Project: Mother's Cafe, Spirit Lake, Iowa, Bob Kloster. Medium: Colored markers, felt pen, and graphite.

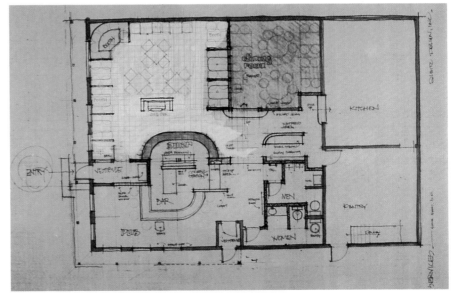

Plate 12

This is an example of a working floor plan as evidenced by the changes made with a solvent wash and cutouts. This floor plan will be coordinated with perspective drawings of specific areas to show the client both the plan and the visual impression of the proposed interior.

Albitz Design, Inc., Minneapolis, MN. Project: Mother's Cafe, Spirit Lake, Iowa, Bob Kloster. Medium: Felt pen and graphite on diazo print.

Plate 13

This perspective view through the rear wall of the cafe towards the diner style dining area uses very little color. The intention of the drawing is to show the organization of the space and the impression made by materials and the interior style.

Albitz Design, Inc., Minneapolis, MN. Project: Cafe, Bob Kloster. Medium: Colored marker, graphite, and felt pen.

Plate 14
Of particular interest in the rendering above is the creation of texture and light with a very loose application of markers. The trees are rendered to be semitransparent to show the playground area, and they also cast light shadows on the ground and roadway. Shadows and changing marker values are used throughout for a feeling of soft light.
Albitz Design, Inc., Minneapolis, MN. Project: Lubavich Learning Center Playground. Medium: Felt pen and marker by Bob Kloster, St. Paul, Minnesota.

Plate 15
This is a crisper drawing than Figure 9-9. Here the line work takes on an added role of value, texture, and shade.
Albitz Design, Inc., Minneapolis, MN. Project: Lubavich Learning Center, St. Paul, Minnesota. Medium: Felt pen, color pencil, and marker by Bob Kloster.

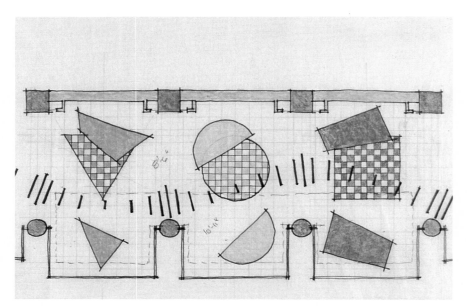

Plate 16
The freehand plan drawing above was done over a light grid to aid accuracy. The drawing was executed to examine product display units, their layout, and the graphic pattern they create in the interior. Plan drawing is one of the three common ways to describe an interior, the other two are perspective or parallel line drawing, and mock-ups or models.
Eva Maddox Associates, Chicago, IL. Project: Haworth. Medium: Felt pen, colored markers, and graphite.

Plate 17
A rough color mockup such as this is an excellent way to visualize the basic forms in the interior. With the addition of color, the graphic patterns and dynamic color relationships are clearly shown. Because the mockup is three dimensional, the color and pattern information is more clearly visualized than on a two dimensional floor plan.
Eva Maddox Associates, Chicago, IL. Project: Haworth. Medium: Colored paper, foam core board, and colored markers.

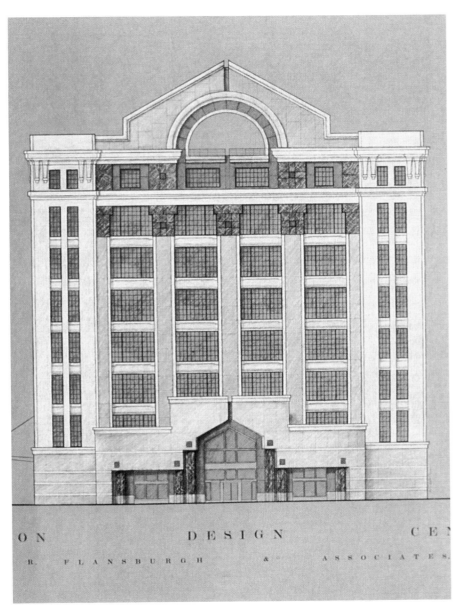

Plate 18

Plate 19

Plates 18 and 19
William Lim, AIA and T. J. Costello, AIA. This rendered print of
an elevation at left illustrates the technique of adding shadows
under edges and at windows to suggest changes in surface
levels. The detail drawing shows the addition of a sky tone.
Earl R. Flansburgh & Associates, Inc., Boston, Ma. Project:
Boston Design Center. Medium: Colored pencil on sepia print.

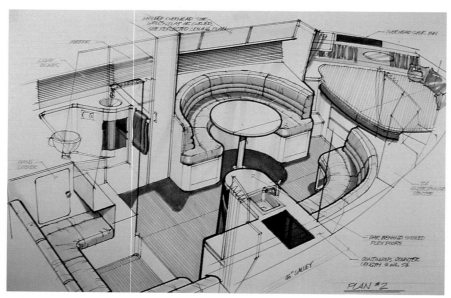

Plate 20

Plates 20, 21, 22, and 23

In the renderings on these two pages, a careful line drawing
is developed and, using drawing guides including a variety of
curves and sweeps, a dark-line drawing is made. Parallel lines
for shading and texture are used as well as various line
weights. Light and dark values are added with markers, and
reflective surfaces indicated by leaving broad areas of white
on rendered surfaces.

Chuck Bednar Design, Oak Park, IL. Client: Doral Boat Company. Medium: Felt pen, marker, chalk, colored pencil on bond paper by Chuck Bednar.

Plate 21

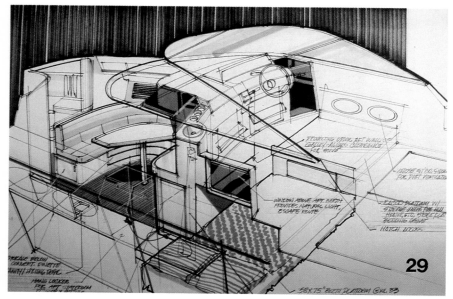

29

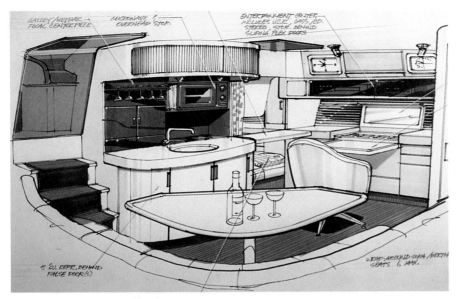

Plate 22

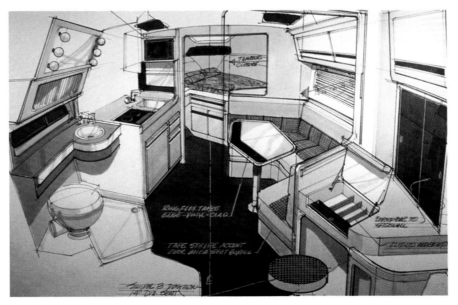

Plate 23

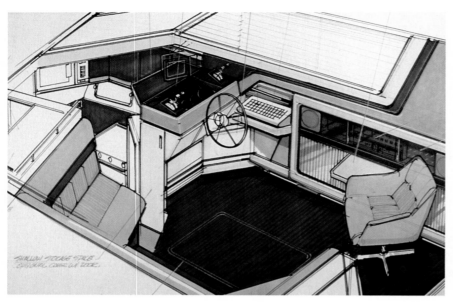

Plate 24
As with the other interior-boat renderings, the exterior lines shown above offer a natural compositional device for the drawings. By looking over and inside, one wall is rendered very little and the dark-solid floor holds the interior together. *Chuck Bednar Design, Oak Park, IL. Client: Cruisers, Inc. Medium: Felt pen, markers, chalk, and colored pencils on layout board by Chuck Bednar.*

Plate 25
The handling of pattern on the floor and seats shows an effective fade-out technique. The lightest values cover much of the area with darks and details only at the focal point. Line work continues throughout the surface to suggest the continuation of the pattern.
Chuck Bednar Design, Oak Park, IL. Client: Skamper Corporation. Medium: Felt pen, marker, chalk, and colored pencil on bond paper by Kurt Mizen.

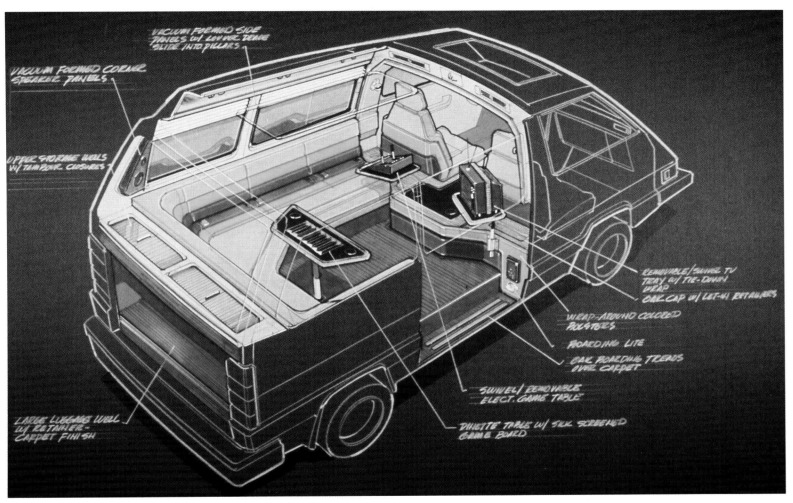

Plate 26

The entire vehicle becomes a background for this interior sketch.

Chuck Bednar Design, Oak Park, IL. Client: Gladiator Van Conversion Company. Medium: Felt pen, marker, chalk, and colored pencil on bond paper by Chuck Bednar.

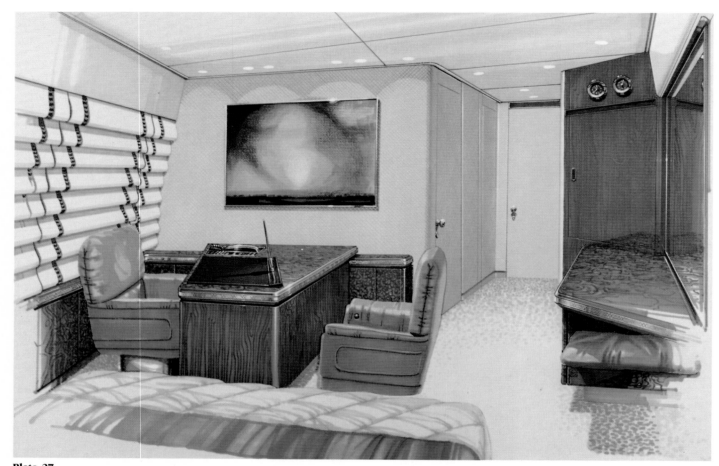

Plate 27

This interior was rendered fairly large (18" x 24") and in great detail. The purpose of the rendering is to show accurately the highly customized interior of a large aircraft, while minimally suggesting the architecture of the aircraft.

Walter Dorwin Teague and Associates, Inc., New York, NY. Project: Aircraft interior. Medium: Colored markers, opaque water-colors on colored illustration board.

9
Portfolio of Professional Work

This chapter contains work from various architectural- and design-consultant offices as well as work from corporate-design offices. Created by designers as part of the design process, these renderings have been selected to show the range of drawing styles and the different roles drawings play from concept development to client presentations, and the range of rendering skills that are effective in the design process. There has been no attempt to present a typical profile of any office represented; rather, drawings have been selected to show a wide range of examples. Along with the drawings are comments about the design office, the project for which the drawing was done, and some comments about the drawing techniques.

Armstrong World Industries
Lancaster, Pennsylvania 17600

Armstrong World Industries designs and manufactures a wide range of high-quality interior architectural products including flooring, acoustical wall paneling, and architectural ceilings. Color plates 7 through 10 represent designs for sets which are built using Armstrong products, which have been photographed and used to advertise their products.

The sketches are loose, depending upon line work to build the perspective and give structure to the surfaces and objects in the interior. Color has been applied to block out the space and suggest the overall decorative feeling of the interior.

Figure 9–1
This is a two-point perspective which is really a one-point perspective in construction as the left-vanishing point is so far out as to make it a minor consideration in the drawing. However, the effect is to have a foreground which is in two-point perspective with the depth and ease of construction of one-point perspective.
Albitz Design Inc., Minneapolis, MN. Project: Albitz-Subshop, Dillingers Diner, Sioux Falls, South Dakota. Medium: India ink, felt pen, graphite on vellum by Bob Kloster.

Figure 9–2a
This shallow, one-point perspective is very much like a stage set. Bold color and silhouettes help the viewer define the space. The layout bond causes the marker to bleed; line work defines the edges of objects. Two values of yellow were used in the ceiling beams to suggest light.
Eva Maddox Associates, Chicago, IL. Project: T. W. Best Newsstand. Medium: Felt-tip pen and markers on layout bond.

Figure 9–2b
The small perspective sketch is really a modified elevation, one of many done to visualize possible graphic arrangements for the space.

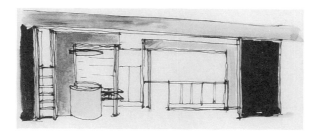

Notice in the sketches that even though the work is quick and loose, shadows, light glare, and value changes have been used to give the impression of light entering the room and to suggest atmosphere. In many instances, a shadow is merely a quick, controlled scribble of gray, and details are strokes of color with some minimal line work.

Albitz Design Inc.
1800 Girard Avenue South
Minneapolis, Minnesota 55403

Albitz Design is a consulting office working out of Minneapolis. The sketches presented in Figure 9-1 and Color plates 11 through 15, like the rest of the project drawings in this text, were done prior to construction. In addition to showing what the project will look like, drawings like these also are used to sell a project. The technique is rough, but the perspective and detailing are accurate to closely reflect the completed job. A mixed application of graphite pencil, markers, felt pens, and india ink was used in the drawings, all of which were done on vellum. In this particular style, bold-line work plays an important role in defining interior element.

Eva Maddox Associates, Inc.
Interior Architecture and Design
440 North Wells
Chicago, Illinois 60610

Figures 9-2a through 9-6 and Color plates 16 and 17 illustrate the work of Eva Maddox Associates, Inc. Eva Maddox Associates was founded in 1975 by Eva L. Maddox, a graduate of the University of Cincinnati's College of Design, Architecture and Art. The Chicago-based firm has since grown to 20 architects and designers who work in teams on a variety of projects. The firm, widely recognized for its showroom and retail designs, is active in select corporate and institutional work. In each project, Eva Maddox Associates strives to maximize the value of design to enhance a product or organization. The firm has received numerous awards and has been profiled extensively in American and European design publications.

Ms. Maddox supports a variety of educational programs and is dedicated to expanding the appreciation of interior architecture as an independent, complementary discipline within the field of architecture. In 1987 she established an Interior Architecture Lectureship at the University of Illinois, and she continues to lecture at other universities and currently serves on advisory committees for the School of the Art Institute of Chicago and the University of Cincinnati. She is active in various professional organizations and is Past Chairman of the Chicago AIA Interiors Committee.

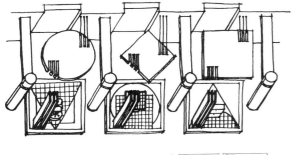

Figure 9–3
This axon study helps visualize the interior space and volumes in relation to the floorplan layout. Axon and perspective drawings are poor choices for showing the graphic patterns in an interior but are good choices to show volume and space relationships.
Eva Maddox Associates, Chicago, IL. Project: Haworth. Medium: Graphite, colored markers, and colored pencils.

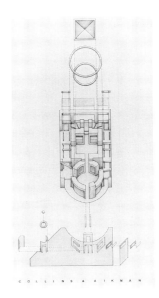

Figure 9–4
This drawing is an exploded axon line drawing based on a floor plan. This type of drawing allows one to see the major interior elements and how they will be positioned in the interior.
Eva Maddox Associates, Chicago, IL. Project: Collins and Aikman. Medium: Colored pencil, ink on colored paper.

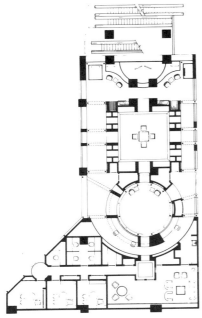

Figure 9–5
This floor plan is lightly rendered to focus the viewers attention on specific areas of the interior plan.
Eva Maddox Associates, Chicago, IL. Project: Collins and Aikman. Medium: Colored pencil and ink.

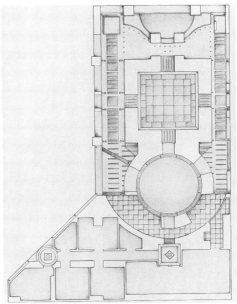

Figure 9–6
This floor plan has been rendered to show the location and suggest the color of the planned carpeting for this interior. Notice the technique to intensify the color at the edges of an area to give better definition to that area, yet keeping the center of the area pale so the drawing holds together and is not fragmented by strong colors.
Eva Maddox Associates, Chicago, IL., Project: Collins and Aikman. Medium: Colored pencil and ink.

Earl R. Flansburgh + Associates, Inc.
77 North Washington Street
Boston, Massachusetts 02114

This firm is a multi-disciplined design firm; its work includes architecture, space planning, interior design, landscape architecture, and graphic design. The work shown here is for a primary/elementary school and a commercial facility. The drawings in Figures 9-7 through 9-10 and Color plates 18 and 19 rely on line work for shape, texture, and value. The play of light plays an important role in defining the interiors.

Figure 9–7
Library Section. This graphite drawing is a one-point perspective based on a section view of the building. Exterior elements are rendered in light values while interior elements are darker and rendered with greater contrast. The strongest indication of light is a highlights washing across the walls by the windows. Otherwise the contrast in the interior makes the drawing read well. Notice some pieces of furniture are drawn as dark silhouettes and some as white plane outlined in black line.
Earl R. Flansburgh + Associates, Inc., Boston, MA. Project: The Park School of Brookline. Delineator: Donald A. Reed, AIA. Figures 9-7, 9-8, 9-9, and 9-10 were part of a package of black-and-white drawings showing different perspective views of the proposed school.

Figure 9–8
Auditorium. In this drawing, the overall dark-and-low-contrast foreground and ceiling lead the viewer to the stage area. It also suggests the dark-audience area.

Figure 9–9
Library, Lower Level. Strong shadows and contrasts increase the impact of this felt-pen drawing. The drawing style is to selectively fill contour lines with a diagonal, carefully-scribbled line. Notice the double shadows under the tables suggesting multiple-light sources.

Figure 9–10
Library. Compare this one-point perspective with Figure 9-8 which is a two-point perspective. The one-point perspective is effective in conveying an idea of the space; however, the composition is not as dramatic.

Paul B. Berger and Associates
Olympia Centre
737 North Michigan Avenue
Suite 1520
Chicago, Illinois 60611
(312) 664-0640

This firm consists of six architects and eight interior designers who concentrate primarily on corporate interior design with clients such as law firms, advertising agencies, real estate developers, and financial organizations.

The drawings in Figures 9-11 through 9-13 are part of a package of plans, details, elevations, and renderings for The Marmon Group's corporate headquarters. It is a two-floor, 36,000-square-foot structure in Chicago's Loop.

Figures 9–11, 9–12, and 9–13
These marker sketches show a simple and effective treatment of floor surfaces. The compositions are rendered to the edge with nearly 100 percent marker coverage. Marker strokes and streaking are used effectively to suggest the structure of the walls and a reflective quality in the floor.
Paul B. Berger and Associates, Chicago, IL. Project: The Marmon Group, Inc.

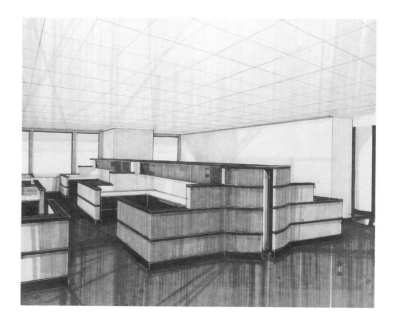

PHH Avenue
303 East Wacker Drive
Chicago, Illinois 60601

The drawings in Figures 9-14 through 9-21 are from a formal presentation series and deal with the interior space of a new building. They are primarily line drawings with some monochrome color for value, shade, and reflections.

Chuck Bednar Design
715 Lake Street
Oak Park, Illinois 60301

Chuck Bednar Design does a significant amount of boat and RV design. The drawings in Color plates 20 through 26 are interiors for those vehicles. This type of interior design is very similar to produce design as the interior is thought of as one interior package, and many of the elements are custom designs. Most of the sketching is in markers, but like any sketch, pencils, prisma colors, and chalk pastels are added at the final stages for finish. Since the exterior architecture of the product is sometimes important as a visual reference to the interior, the underlay often includes both the interior and exterior form lines. Details of the sketch are rendered from the inside out and end when enough of the interior has been defined; this may include some show-through of the exterior line.

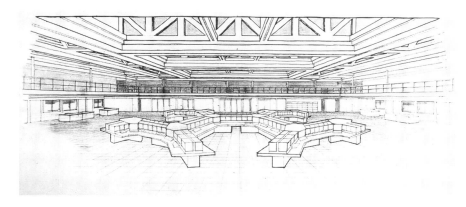

Figure 9–14
Trading room, south side.

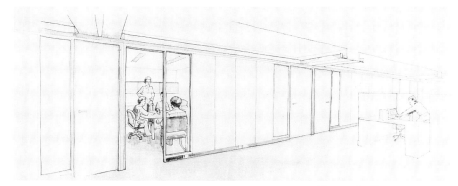

Figure 9–15
Corridor at office fronts.

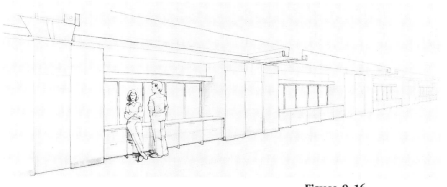

Figure 9–16
Corridor at windows.

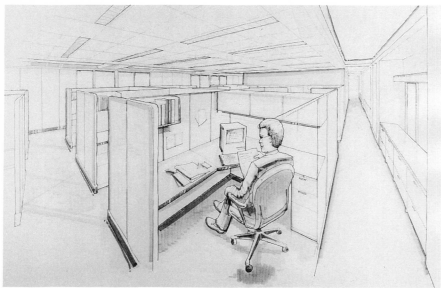

Figure 9-17
Annex.

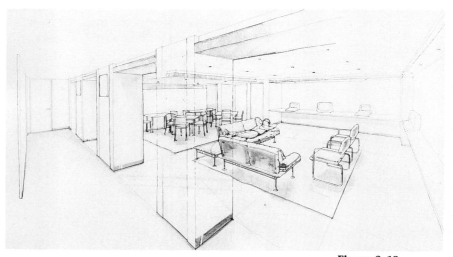

Figure 9-18
Market makers lounge.

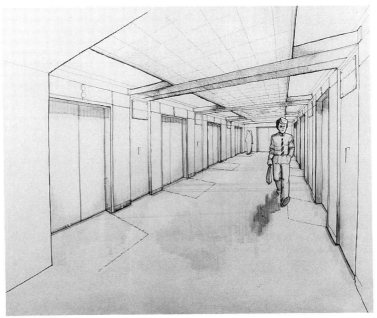

9-19
Elevator lobby.

Figure 9-20
Corridor at demising wall.

Figure 9-21
Reception at annex. Drawings 9-14 through 9-21 are very consistent in format and execution. A variety of line weights are used to help the viewer read different planes in space. The light, warm values on the drawings suggest reflections and shadows as well as make the space to seem more inviting. Notice in Figure 9-18 the transparent pillar allowing the viewer to see into the lounge area.
PHH Avenue, Chicago, IL. Project: O'Connor and Associates. Medium: Ink and marker on vellum.

Figure 9-22
This line drawing has been minimally rendered using light, neutral values. The viewer is drawn into the space over the trading floor to the strong red stripe on the back wall.
Space/Management Programs, Inc., Chicago, IL. Project: Trading floors. Medium: Ink, marker.

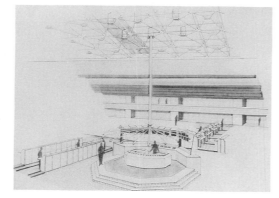

Space/Management Programs, Inc.
230 North Michigan Avenue
Chicago, Illinois 60601-5971

This firm has done an extensive amount of work for financial-exchange markets such as the Chicago Board of Trade, Chicago Mercantile Exchange, and the Pacific Stock Exchange, Inc. The drawings shown in Figures 9-22 through 9-24 show some typical considerations in the design of a trade center.

Walter Dorwin Teague and Associates
Executive Offices
95 Madison Avenue
New York, New York 10016

Figure 9-23
This is a line perspective on yellow trace to show the layout of a trading floor. Light-gray values have been added with marker to the shade areas.
Space/Management Programs, Inc., Chicago, IL. Project: Trading floors. Medium: Ink, marker.

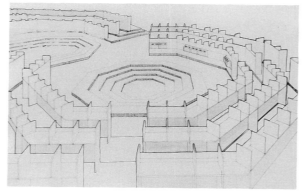

Teague Associates is a very large consulting firm involved in all aspects of design and maintaining offices in New York, Seattle, Renton, Everett, and Washington, D.C. Their offices in the state of Washington have, in addition to other design work, a long history of transportation design including a considerable number of aircraft interiors. Examples of the Teague Associates' elaborate renderings are shown in Figures 9-25 and 9-26.

Perkins and Will
123 North Wacker Drive
Chicago, Illinois 60606

Figure 9-24
This sightline elevation makes use of strong silhouettes and high contrast to increase visual interest.
Space/Management Programs, Inc., Chicago, IL. Project: Trading floors. Medium: Ink, marker.

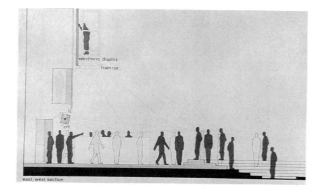

Perkins and Will is a full service architectural, engineering, planning, and interior architecture firm. The project shown in Figures 9-27 through 9-35 was completed for Stotler + Company of Chicago in 1987. The design team consisted of:

Neil P. Frankel, AIA, Vice President/Design Principal
Neena Konon, Project Manager
James E. Prendergast, AIA, Senior Project Designer
Julie DePrey, Project Designer
Billy Tindell, Project Designer

The Problem. This financial-futures client required expansion of its facilities at the Chicago Board of Trade (CBOT). The client elected to relocate its corporate headquarters to a downtown-Chicago high-rise while maintaining trading functions at the CBOT.

The Solution. The 40,000-square-foot office is an elegant expression of the client's desire for a tasteful environment which establishes a professional corporate identity and permits a functional work atmosphere. The upscale tone of the space is set from the moment one enters the executive office area on the 24th floor: Visitors arrive into a mahogany-paneled elevator lobby, accented by a solid-beige carpet which is framed in two types of marble. Sliding-glass doors, etched with a grid-like stencil pattern, open into a formal reception area featuring an artistically-modified commodities quotation machine on a glass-covered marble pedestal.

Adjacent to the reception area, a set of wood and etched-glass doors provides access to the executive office corridor. The extensive length of this passageway is visually modulated through the placement of alcove-like nodes flanked by marble columns which form distinct entrances to paired doorways along the corridor. Above each node, domed and pyramidal-recessed ceilings identify individual offices or group-meeting areas. Workstations for secretaries are located at either end of the executive area, across from the partner offices.

Within the executive corridor is the corporate boardroom, complete with a projection screen, a mahogany and marble conference table with leather chairs, and an adjacent dining-conference area. The etched-glass door of the boardroom provides a privacy screen while it permits natural light to penetrate the interior areas.

The executive floor of the office is also home to the company's legal and marketing-research departments. Due to the high office traffic generated in these areas, carpet tiles were selected to provide a durable and attractive floor covering. Ambient lighting over individual workstations helps to diffuse glare for employees working at computer terminals.

By integrating contemporary materials with those of a more traditional palette, the office of Stotler + Company is reflective of both the company's newly-expanded service offerings and its long-standing reputation of excellence in the area of financial futures.

Figure 9–25
This is a very elaborate interior rendering which accuately describes the surface textures, colors and patterns to be used in the interior. The walls and ceiling are minimally rendered, relying heavily on line work and fading out to the edges of the drawing to frame the fully rendered interior elements. Notice the strong contrasts used between the highlight top surfaces, shade surfaces and the shadow areas.
Walter Dorwin Teague and Associates. Project: Aircraft Interior. Medium: Ink, felt markers, opaque watercolors on colored illustration board.

Figure 9–26
Because the shell of commercial aircraft changes little from one plane to another the focus of this rendering is upon the elements that can easily be changed to create a new interior. Therefore the seats, carpet, and partitions are carefully detailed. The walls and ceiling are suggested by minimal line work and color.
Walter Dorwin Teague and Associates. Project: Aircraft Interior. Medium: Ink, colored markers, opaque watercolors on illustration board.

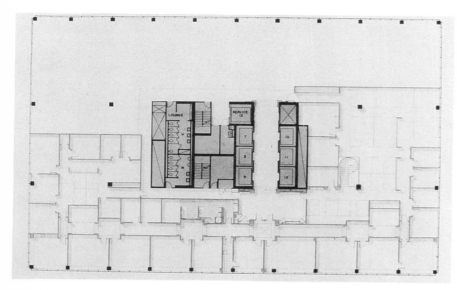

Figure 9–27

Final-presentation floor plan which contains the executive offices. This plan was done in pencil on mylar, to allow corrections to be made and to produce clear copies. The floor plan serves as the main drawing in a presentation which is supported by other drawings.

Perkins and Will, Chicago, IL. Project: Strotler & Company Corporate Offices.

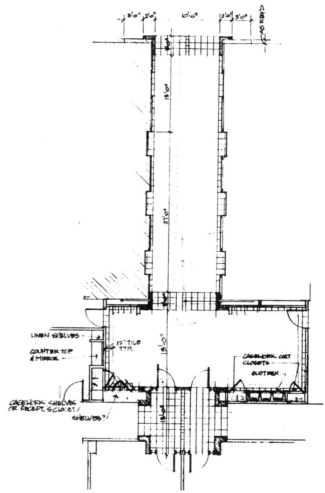

Figure 9–28

Elevator-lobby plan done in pencil on white trace. This dimensioned study helps to "fix" the size and location of interior components.

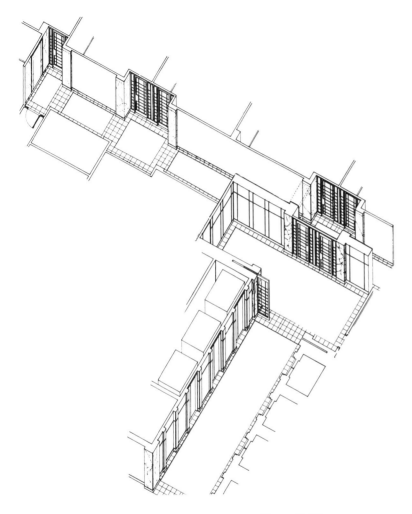

Figure 9-29
This finished axonometric drawing was done with pencil, ink, and colored pencil on white trace. It was used as a presentation drawing to the client.

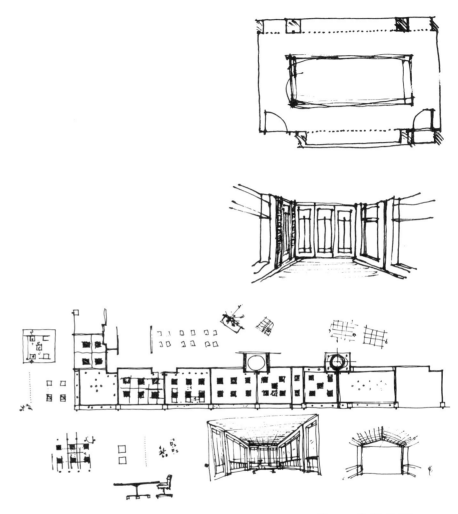

Figures 9-30, 9-31
Conference-room sketches done in felt-tip pen on white trace. These are typical early-design sketches used to visualize and plan the interior space.

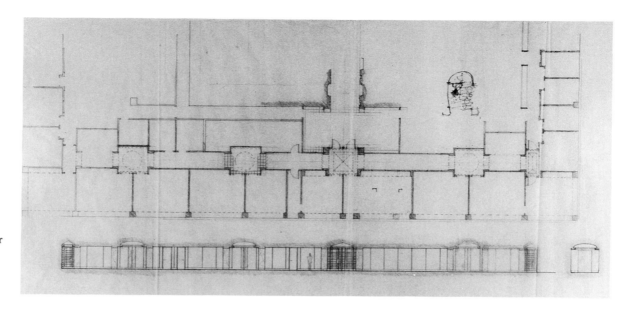

Figure 9-32
Executive-corridor analysis done in pencil and colored pencil on white trace. This type of drawing is done after the loose study sketches to ensure the design concepts are workable and appropriate.

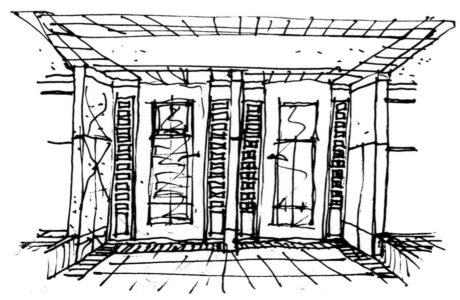

Figure 9-33
Earliest concept of entrance modules as nodes which would become a theme throughout the interior. This sketch is done in ink on yellow trace.

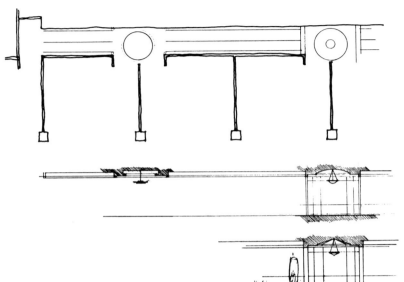

Figure 9-34
A study of volume and space for the entrance nodes done in pencil on white trace.

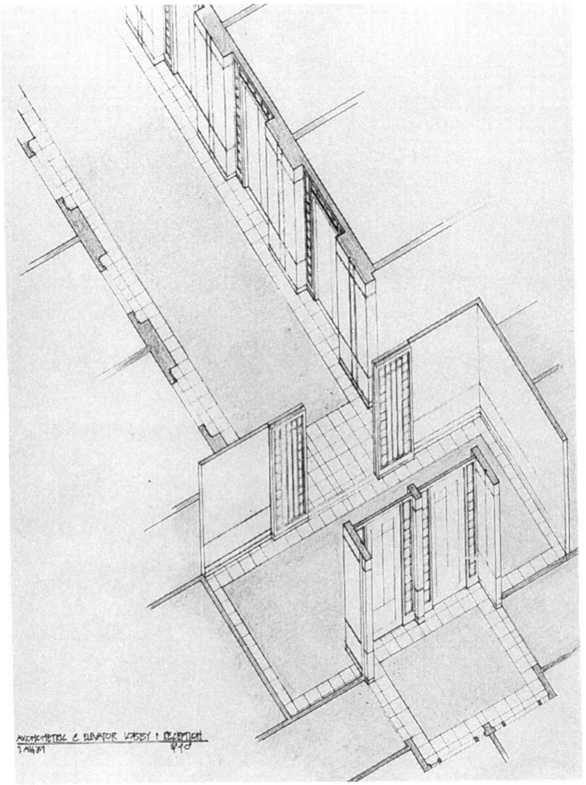

Figure 9-35
Axonometric of entrance node done in pencil and ink on white trace.

Appendix: Materials Used in Color Rendering

BRIDGES

A bridge is a specialized guide for use with a paintbrush which is usually straight with feet at either end to span over the drawing without touching it. The edge is raised high enough off of the paper surface that the ferrule of the brush runs along the bridge's edge. The designer's fingers lightly run across the top of the bridge to control the touch of the brush on the paper, thus determining the line width. To achieve shaped lines, another guide may be placed on the bridge with the desired shape extending over the edge of the bridge to run the brush along.

BRUSHES

Of a paintbrush's parts, the bristles, a metal ferrule, and a wooden handle, the bristles are the most important part; one should therefore get a good-quality sable brush. Sable brushes keep a tip well, carry and hold a good body of pigment, and are responsive. The brush is used primarily for high-lighting and lettering, both of which require a fine point such as 0 or 00. One may want to get a fine-lettering brush as well with a chiseled tip which produces an even, flat stroke for lettering or wide highlights.

COLORED PENCILS

Colored pencils are very good for detailing small areas, adding highlights, and adding a color tone to part of a drawing. A fairly soft, wax-base pencil and a wide selection of colors are recommended for rendering. The pencils need to be handled with care as dropping an unsharpened pencil on a hard floor may crack the lead inside, a rough pencil sharpener may continually "chew up" the point, and the leads will break easily. An electric pencil sharpener is very handy for keeping a good point and will save time. When purchasing colored pencils, select a color palette from both the warm and cool ranges and include accent colors like violet and pink. Check the end of the pencil to see if the lead is well centered; if not, the pencil will not sharpen to a good point.

Colored pencils are essentially transparent and may be used in three ways. The first method uses a sharp point either to tighten up edges, to add highlights, or to put in thin accent lines. These thin lines are often ruled in along a triangle or guide. A helpful technique when ruling is to twirl the pencil as it is run along the edge to keep a point and prevent the line from getting fat and vague.

A white pencil is commonly used for highlights along edges and in de-tails; however, in dark areas, a silver pencil will do a better job; the white pencil is dulled by the dark-marker dye while the reflective silver picks up room light and gives added sparkle to the highlight. A thin line of warm-accent color (e.g., light yellow) along the highlight edge will crisp up the highlight and make the surface seem more reflective as well as add a tint of color to create a sense of light and atmosphere about the rendering. A cool-accent color (e.g., lilac) can be put in the shade area along the halo to crisp up and cool the back edge of the rendering.

The second manner in which colored pencils are used is to tone an area. By using an underhand grip on the pencil, the side of the lead can be rubbed over an area imparting a thin, transparent tone which can alter the color, put a glow on a surface, or warm or cool areas. Be sure to have a smooth surface under the marker paper as any texture will be picked up by the pencils.

The third use for colored pencils is to add small details, built up with successive layers of the transparent color, working in highlights and shade areas. By blending the colors together with a white, light gray, or cream pencil and then adding a final layer of color, the intensity is increased and a smooth, uniform surface is left. The edges of the detail can be tightened up with a fine, dark pencil or pen and also markers can be worked over color pencil. They melt the pencil and blend it which dulls and tints the pencil color; however, markers should not be overused or the area will become muddy, and the pencil will have to be cleaned out of the marker tip by stroking the marker on a sheet of scratch paper as the wax from the pencils may clog the marker's nib.

DRAWING PENCILS AND LEADS

Two types of drawing pencils are available: the common wood-lead pencil and the mechanical pencil which accepts a variety of leads. The leads for mechanical pencils range from hard to soft and from a large to a very fine point (.3mm). These fine leads are nice for drafting and linework as they do not need sharpening, and the larger leads are better for drawing as they can put down more graphite quickly and with a variety of line weights.

Pencil leads come in a range of hardness from 6B (very soft) to 9H (very hard). A middle range of pencil leads works well for most rendering. Soft leads, such as 2B or HB, produce bold, dark lines for lettering and some shading. F and H are medium-soft leads which keep a fine point for detailing and tightening up lettering. A 2H lead is medium-hard, the same as a common lead pencil, and is good for light-line drawings and layout work. A pencil with a very soft lead, 6B, can give a very dark line and is good for quick-value studies. Because soft leads put down so much graphite, they smear easily if a hand is run over them so it is a good idea to slip a piece of paper under the palm to prevent smudging.

ELLIPSE GUIDES

A circle in perspective is drawn as an ellipse. Depending upon the angle from which one is viewing the circle, it will appear as anywhere from a very narrow ellipse to a very full, "round" ellipse. Ellipse guides come in a series of 5 degree increments, from a narrow 10° ellipse to a wide 80° ellipse. The guides also come in two sets, one from ⅛ inch to 2 inches and the other from 2⅛ inches to 4 inches. Having access to both sets of ellipse guides is very helpful when rendering because freehand ellipses are difficult to draw and are seldom convincing.

ERASERS

A number of different erasers are available; only two types, however, are needed in rendering, a kneaded eraser and a "Pink Pearl." The kneaded eraser is soft and pliable and will remove large amounts of pencil or chalk from a drawing. When the eraser becomes dirty, it can be kneaded clean. The advantages of the kneaded eraser are that it does not leave crumbs and can be shaped to a point to pick out details.

The "Pink Pearl" is a soft, rubber eraser that removes lines the kneaded eraser will not remove. It comes in varying degrees of hardness, and because all hard erasers tend to rough up the paper, it is recommended that the designer use a soft pink eraser. The pink eraser may also be used to "draw" light lines in chalked areas by erasing lines in the chalk. This eraser is cleaned by rubbing it on a piece of scrap paper.

ERASING SHIELDS

A typical erasing shield is a small, rectangular piece of metal with a variety of shaped holes cut into it through which one can erase. For rendering it may be necessary to erase up to or along an edge; to do this, a piece of paper may be laid down as a shield.

FLEXIBLE CURVES

Flexible curves are strips of metal or plastic that may be bent into almost any gentle curve. These guides allow one to rule a fine or broad line on irregular contours. Kinks commonly develop in these curves when they are handled roughly or when one tries to make a tight corner. Once a kink develops, the curve is of little use for accurate lines, so they should be handled carefully. To use the curve, it is twisted into roughly the desired shape and positioned on the paper. Holding it firmly with one hand, it is adjusted to the exact curve desired while the line is ruled with the other hand.

GUIDES

Another way to control an otherwise loose application of color is to use a guide. This is simply a shaped pattern that guides the marker or other tool along its edge. The most common guides are a triangle, circle, ellipse guide and a T square. When used with markers, the guides must be held slightly above the paper surface so the dye will not bleed under the guide. This may be done by taping a thin piece of cardboard to the underside of the guide just in from the edge. A dime can be taped under the guide to "lift" it. The marker is then either drawn along the edge of the guide or butted up to it in a series of rapid strokes. A very convenient guide for marking straight lines is a piece of matboard. The marker can be run along the edge without the dye bleeding underneath. Matboard is also disposable, with no need to clean the edges after each use.

Guides are also very effective when spraying color to block an area or to control an edge when spraying color. Note when spraying color that the further from the paper surface the guide is held, the fuzzier the edge of the line becomes, an advantage that masks do not have.

LIGHT TABLE

A light table is a useful tool for refining, tightening up, or modifying a line drawing. It consists of a series of lights arranged under a white, translucent surface. Preliminary line drawings may be taped down and the lines "projected" through a clean sheet laid over the drawing, and using a light pencil, the projected lines may be traced or changed as desired. When the light table is turned off, the lines from the underlay vanish leaving a new drawing free from distracting lines and ready for further work.

MARKERS

There are several brands of art markers, and the range of colors offered by each marker brand varies greatly. Some sets have very bright, intense colors that are good for graphic design and layout work, while other sets include a wide range of muted tones that are necessary for rendering. Selecting a palette of markers can be time-consuming, as each marker must be tested and compared to other markers to judge its hue, value, and intensity. Then a series of compatible markers for each desired color must be selected.

But once a color palette is defined, using the markers becomes much easier and the selection much quicker. It is recommended that the markers in any given color series be numbered one through five (or however many markers are in the series) from light to dark, for quick-value reference.

The following are suggested monochromatic palettes for making quick presentation sketches, although they will need to be augmented with accent and highlight colors. Each palette list ranges from a very light value through a bright hue color to a dark shade of that color. Quick pencil/marker value sketching can be done using the darkest marker in a series and a matching Prismacolor color pencil.

Chartpak AD Markers

YELLOW SERIES

133 Maze
 41 Lemon yellow
 42 Cadmium yellow
 43 Dark yellow
 47 Gold

Prismacolor pencil #942 Yellow Ochre
Colorama pencil #8033 Gold ochre

BLUE SERIES

105 Ice blue
103 Sky blue
 5 True blue
 9 Airforce blue
 7 Navy blue

Prismacolor pencil #901 Indigo
Colorama pencil #8025 Indigo

ORANGE SERIES

62 Chrome orange
63 Amber
65 Sanguine
66 Saffron
75 Burnt sienna

Prismacolor pencil #944 Terra cotta
Colorama pencil #8013 Terra cotta

"COOL" RED SERIES

163 Pink
168 Shadow pink
83 Ruby
84 Rubine red
85 Maroon

Prismacolor pencil #925 Crimson
lake
Colorama pencil #8076 Lake red

VIOLET SERIES

177 Mauve
178 Purple sage
96 Blueberry
94 Violet
1 Blue violet

Prismacolor pencil #932 Violet
Colorama pencil #8024 Violet

"COOL" BLUE SERIES

112 Frost blue
111 Pale veridian
113 Arctic blue
15 Process blue
13 Peacock blue

Prismacolor pencil #903 True blue
Colorama pencil #8015 Cobalt blue

GREEN SERIES

122 Grass green
32 Palm green
29 Leaf green
25 Jade
21 Emerald green

Prismacolor pencil #907 peacock
green
Colorama pencil #8058 Virid green

Berol Prismacolor Art Markers

YELLOW SERIES

23 Cream
20 Process yellow
19 Canary yellow
18 Cadmium yellow
17 Yellow orange
22 Mustard
or 69 Yellow ochre

pencil #942 Yellow ochre

ORANGE SERIES

15 Orange
16 Bittersweet
14 Vermilion
13 Chinese vermilion
 2 Chinese red

pencil #925 Crimson lake

RED SERIES

10 Blush
 9 Apple blossom
 6 Scarlet
 5 Scarlet lake
 2 Chinese red
or 4 Crimson

pencil #925 Crimson lake

MAGENTA SERIES

 8 Pink
 1 Process red
54 Magenta
53 Purple
52 Cranberry

pencil #931 Purple

VIOLET SERIES

60 Light violet
50 Violet
49 Blue violet

pencil #932 Violet

TAN SERIES

96 Blond wood
70 Sand
or
78 Brick beige
80 Putty

BROWN SERIES

89 Light walnut
84 Bark
88 Walnut
63 Dark brown

pencil #947 Burnt umber

GREEN SERIES

25 Chartreuse
29 True green
28 Nile green
34 Olive green
33 Marine green
or 31 Dark green and
pencil #908 Dark green

pencil #911 Olive green

BLUE SERIES

48 Non-photo blue
39 Process blue
40 True blue
44 Ultramarine
45 Indigo blue
or 43 Copenhagen blue

pencil #901 Indigo blue

RED BROWN SERIES

71 Beige
95 Light tan
94 Dark tan

Mecanorma Art Markers

MAGENTA SERIES

132 Ice pink
269 Pale pink
131 Pink
120 Magenta

RED SERIES

289 Cherry pink
137 Coral
242 Middle red
124 Red
125 Cadmium
181 Red wood

YELLOW BROWN SERIES

184 Sand
185 Buff
290 Gold brown
182 Walnut
239 Sepia

GREEN SERIES

179 Pale green
167 Forest green
166 Middle green
252 Second green
164 Deep green
169 Emerald

ORANGE SERIES

116 Pale orange
112 Orange
111 Deep orange

YELLOW SERIES

288 Ice naple
195 Ice yellow
106 Middle yellow
105 Deep yellow
235 Gold ochre

RED BROWN SERIES

115 Lt. salmon
270 Mahogany light
266 Mahogany
259 Burnt umber
262 Dark brown

ICE BLUE SERIES

206 Ice blue
205 Pale sky blue
203 Sky blue
202 Blue
151 Indigo

BLUE SERIES

149 Pale blue
245 Cobalt blue light
144 Cobalt blue
143 Ultramarine
264 Prussian blue

MASKS

Masking is an effective technique for getting crisp edges around quickly rendered areas of a drawing; it is done for either marker, chalk, or dyes. It is used in rendering in two ways: to block out and keep white a small area that can be rendered around and over, and to mask around a large area that then can be rendered quickly and loosely.

Unless the area to be masked has straight edges and sharp corners on which masking tapes can be applied directly, the mask will need to be cut and shaped to the desired contour. To avoid cutting through the marker paper, either render on a heavy board (e.g., illustration board) or precut the mask before applying it to the rendering. Precutting is done easily by using a translucent mask material (frisket or tracing paper), laying it over the rendering, and tracing the lines to be cut. Lay the translucent mask material over a smooth cutting surface and carefully cut along the trace lines, and then position the mask on the rendering and apply the color.

When markers are used, the mask must adhere firmly to the paper at the edge or the marker dye will bleed under the mask. The adhesive may be discolored by the marker base and leave stains or may be too tacky and tear the paper or pull up the color under it. Several good masking materials are available, but frisket is perhaps the best for cutting out shaped areas. Tracing paper works well if one is only stroking away from the mask or if using dry chalk. Any unwanted chalk may be removed with a Pink Pearl eraser.

For straight edges and angular corners, many tapes can be used. Scotch 811 tape is very good and will not tear marker paper and is also easy to cut corners and shape details by lifting the edge and lightly cutting the tape with a sharp #11 X-acto blade. Another good mask for marker paper is the wax-backed painter's mask found in most hardware stores. It has a light tack, yet bonds well at the edge and does not leave a residue on the paper.

MORGUE FILE

A morgue file, as noted in Chapter 2, is a convenient source file of reference materials for both the beginner and the experienced renderer. It may contain photographs of things to draw from, examples of specific details or materials that are troublesome to render, or images of people and support elements to put into a rendering for scale and interest. Be very selective in what is put into the file and continue to build and edit it. It is a valuable tool. The following is a suggested list for building a file:

▶ A collection of photographs of interiors to draw from and refer to for details, reflections, highlights, and transitions. Select a clear, well-defined photograph rather than an overly dramatic or shadowed one.

▶ Examples of rendering and sketching techniques from both printed material and original work. These can be a source for growth and help to demonstrate how others solved certain problems.

▶ A people file of both casual sketches and photographic examples. Some anatomical and ergonomic references also are helpful here. Avoid excessively stylized and distorted fashion illustrations.

▶ A general catch-all file of things of interest.

▶ A file of technical drawings and diagrams.

OPAQUE WHITE

Opaque white is a water-base paint that covers markers, pencil, and ink without bleeding. It may be used with a brush, a technical pen, or an air-brush for two main purposes: to put in highlights and to put in light details. When light details are desired on a dark ground, the opaque white is put down with the light color over it. One should be cautious if detailing with a water-based fineline dark pen because putting white opaque over it will melt the color, which, in turn, will contaminate the white opaque. Always thin the opaque to the consistency of heavy cream so that it flows well from the brush or pen; it has a tendency to thicken and glob.

PAPER

The most common papers used for rendering are listed below. Each paper has unique characteristics but, with a little experience, they are all fairly easy to work with.

Colored Papers

This includes mat board, canson colored paper, and quality cover-stock papers. Because colored papers require the additional set-up procedure of transferring the line drawing to the colored paper, and because colored papers are not a common working paper for designers, drawings done on colored paper are perceived as slightly more formal, definitely not as working sketches. Colored papers take markers, chalk, colored pencil, and paint very well and are a good choice for elaborate renderings.

Marker Paper and Layout Board

These are the typical white papers designers use day in and day out. They are good for sketches and can be rendered on with excellent results. Because the paper is thin, it can be traced through for working from underlays. The quality to look for in these types of paper is how much bleeding the markers do. The designer can select the one he or she is comfortable with.

Reproduction Papers

These are usually absorbent papers that bleed a lot; hence they require heavy-line work to define interior elements. The greatest advantage they offer is the ease of reproduction of line drawings by photocopying or diazo processes. The reproductions can be rendered or modified and rendered as desired.

Tracing Papers and Vellum

Using transparent paper for sketching requires special handling when making a presentation to prevent the background from showing through. Inexpensive trace comes in white or yellow, popular for its pleasing tone and its ability to modify markers to a slightly warmer, less-intense color. They do not hold up well for elaborate renderings or for much color work, although high-quality tracing papers like vellum are excellent papers for rendering. They do not accept wet media such as designers' watercolors very well.

PASTELS AND CHALK

The extent to which pastels and chalk can be used in a rendering depends upon the paper being used. Chalk will not adhere to hard, smooth papers like marker paper but will take very nicely to toothy or soft papers like canson or diazo paper. Chalks are generally used for backgrounds, for toning areas, and for adding highlights or glare to a rendering.

Chalks can be used dry or dissolved with thinner on a cotton pad. As a dry medium, the chalk may be stroked directly onto the paper from the square stick which leaves a hard edge to the chalk, advantageous when rendering highlights and glare. To tone an area, the chalk should be powdered by scraping with a blade and rubbed on the rendering with a cotton pad. When rubbing the chalk, it is helpful to use masks and an eraser may be used to clean up edges or "draw" light lines in the chalk.

To use chalk as a wet medium, powder it, and use a cotton pad dipped in thinner (rubber cement thinner or lighter fluid) to pick up the chalk and stroke it on the rendering. When used wet, chalk is difficult to remove, so careful masking is important.

Here are a few guidelines for using chalk in a marker rendering.

► Like markers, chalks should be applied directly without repeated handling. Put a stroke down and leave it. Overworking an area makes for a smudged, muddy rendering.

► When chalk colors are mixed, they lose their brilliance. This is to one's advantage in backgrounds where more subdued colors are desired. Also, incomplete mixing causes streaking, which can be a nice effect. For highlights and toning, however, the colors should be kept pure and bright.

► Chalks smudge easily and will melt and muddy when markers are applied over them. They also tend to clog marker tips. Therefore, the chalk should be put on a rendering at the very end after all the other work is done. Spraying fixative over chalk darkens the color and, in some cases, softens the marker enough to allow it to blend with the chalk. When this occurs, the chalk color is no longer visible.

► If chalks need to be applied to a marker paper, the surface must be prepared. Rubbing the paper with talc, even over markers, will allow the chalk to adhere to the surface better.

► To remove large amounts of chalk, a kneaded eraser is used to blot up most of the chalk, and then a soft pink eraser is used to remove the final bits of color.

► Chalk sticks may be shaped on fine sandpaper to control their width and to keep a sharp edge.

RAPIDOGRAPHS

Rapidograph is a brand name commonly used to refer to all hollow-point technical drawing pens which come in a range of point sizes from .13 mm to 2 mm. The very fine points are designated by zeros, five times zero ("00000") being the finest, and increasing in size through four times zero ("0000"), three times zero, "00", and "0," all the way to 6. They all produce a very sharp, uniform line. Used primarily for technical drawing, these pens are also excellent for detailing a rendering. They use a waterproof, black ink. Although colored inks are available, the difficulty of changing inks makes using them impractical, although it may be wise to consider keeping one pen for use with white ink for some highlights and white linework. The major problem with Rapidographs is that the ink tends to dry and clog the tip. There is little one can do to prevent this, although the newer pens have good seals in the caps and dry out very slowly.

T SQUARES

A T square slides along the edge of the drawing board, allowing a designer to rule a series of horizontal, parallel lines. Triangles can be set on the edge of a T square to rule vertical or angular lines and should have a raised or beveled edge to prevent bleeding under it as one rules lines or strokes markers along its edge.

THINNERS AND SOLVENTS

Solvents such as rubber-cement thinner, naphtha, acetone, lighter fluid, and xylene are very volatile and can be dangerous so a spill-proof dispenser, such as an "oil can" rubber-cement-thinner dispenser, is recommended to prevent spilling. Solvents are useful for wetting a cloth or cotton pad to clean marker dye off drafting tools. They also are used for special effects and for blending markers and chalk. When rendering on vellum, a solvent pad can be used to erase or pick up marker color from the paper. Some art material companies offer special solvents for their products in prepackaged dispensers. Two common universal solvents for markers are rubber cement thinner and lighter fluid.

TRANSFER PAPER

To transfer a line drawing to an opaque surface (illustration board or canson), a transfer sheet, which is a sheet similar to carbon paper, is slipped between the drawing and the new surface. The line drawing is then redrawn using firm pressure, causing the chalky powder on the transfer paper to mark the lines on the opaque surface. The lines of this transfer drawing are not permanent and may be erased easily. However, they also resist smudging, making them clean and easy to work with. An alternate method of transferring a drawing is to rub the back of the original line drawing with colored chalk or colored pencil (metallic pencils work well also). This is a more time-consuming technique, and the chalk method can be messy. Both the transfer-paper lines and the chalk lines are easy to remove from the paper surface and, when drawn over with marker, tend to dissolve. The metallic pencil lines do not readily dissolve, but they are light and can be seen only when looked at from an angle; they are not evident in the final rendering.

TRIANGLES

There are two basic triangles, a 45-degree triangle and a 30-60 degree triangle. You will need one of both. Aside from using them for the traditional drafting tasks, triangles are useful as straight-edges for tightening up a rendering and as guides to run markers along. Of the two triangles, the 30-60 degree triangle is the most convenient for rendering because it covers less surface area for the same length hypotenuse. Therefore, it is less awkward to move about the drawing board when used as a straightedge.

The transparent acrylic triangles have two advantages over other triangles: first, they can be seen through, making positioning easier; second, the edge does not crack or get sticky when it is cleaned with marker solvent. As with all guides, the edge of the triangle should be raised or beveled to prevent bleeding.

It is advisable to have a number of different size triangles. The most commonly used is a 12-inch triangle, measured along the longest leg. This size is sufficient for most rendering and layout work.

ANNOTATED BIBLIOGRAPHY

Arends, Mark. **Product Rendering with Markers**. New York: Van Nostrand Reinhold Company, 1985.
As the title suggests this text is concerned with product rendering. It is very thorough and explains in detail the use of markers in rendering.

Ching, Francis D. K. **Interior Design Illustrated**. New York: Van Nostrand Reinhold Company, 1987.
A comprehensive introduction to interior design, explaining the basic issues of interior design with text and illustrations.

D'Amelio, Joseph. **Perspective Drawing Handbook**. New York: Van Nostrand Reinhold Company, 1984.
Explains and illustrates the concepts of perspective and the choices and techniques available to the designer in laying out drawings.

Doblin, Jay. **Perspective: A New System for Designers**. New York: Watson Guptill Publications, 1956.
Presents a very good system for quickly setting up and drawing in perspective. Allows for combination of mechanical and freehand drawing.

Doyle, Michael. **Color Drawing**. New York: Van Nostrand Reinhold Company, 1981.
A very good manual for architectural rendering with markers and colored pencils.

Gill, Robert. **The VNR Manual of Rendering with Pen and Ink**, rev. ed. New York: Van Nostrand Reinhold Company, 1984.
Provides techniques of using Rapidographs and ink pens for architectural black-and-white rendering.

Hanks, Kurt, and Belliston, Larry. **Draw!: A Visual Approach to Thinking, Learning, and Communicating**. Los Altos: William Kauffman, Inc., 1977.
This book helps develop skills in idea sketching and using thumbnails as effective thinking tools.

Hanks, Kurt, and Belliston, Larry. **Rapid Viz: A New Method for Rapid Visualization of Ideas**. Los Altos: William Kauffman, Inc., 1980.
This is a how-to formula for sketching ideas. It does not go into presentation sketches or marker techniques.

Kemnitzer, Ronald B. **Rendering with Markers**. New York: Watson-Guptill Publications, 1983.
This text shows the basic marker technique for rendering a variety of subjects from products to architecture.

Leach, Sid. **Techniques of Interior Design Rendering and Presentation**. New York: McGraw Hill, Inc., 1978.
A very good how-to manual for interior rendering and making presentations. The techniques and rendering medium are suitable for an illustrator.

Leinbach, Richard B. **Visualization Techniques**. Englewood Cliffs, New Jersey: Prentice-Hall, Inc., 1986.
An instructional text showing procedures for setting up axonometric drawings, one- and two-point perspectives and making three-dimensional models.

Martin, C. Leslie. **Design Graphics**, 2nd ed. New York: Macmillan, Inc., 1968.
Technical drafting manual for orthographics, paraline drawing, perspective, shadows, and some rendering. Easy to understand and thorough.

Munsell, A. H. **A Color Notation**. Baltimore: Munsell Color Company, Inc.
Comes with student color charts and a color wheel. Explains the Munsell color system very clearly.

Powell, Dick. **Design Rendering Techniques**. London: Orbis Publishing Ltd., 1985.
A very well illustrated text on product-rendering techniques.

Powell, Dick, and Monahan, Patricia. **Marker Rendering Techniques**. London: MacDonald and Co., Ltd., 1987.
A well-illustrated text showing marker techniques for illustration, advertising, textiles, packaging, interior and product design, and film.

Ramsay, C. G., and Sleeper, H. R., eds. **Architectural Graphic Standards**, 7th ed. New York: John Wiley & Sons, Inc., 1981.
This manual details the appropriate technical graphic representation for specifying architectural features. It includes standards for all aspects of architectural design from furniture plans to mechanical specifications and construction details.

Welling, Richard. **Drawing with Markers**. New York: Watson Guptill Publications, 1974.
A manual for using markers in a free-sketch style. Includes landscapes, still lifes, etc.

Index